Ward Sisters—
Another Perspective

Their Ongoing Educational Needs

MARY F. STAPLETON
M.Phil., Dip. Ed. Research (Surrey), DHSA (Aston)),
RGN, SCM

AIMS OF THE SERIES

To encourage the appreciation and dissemination of nursing research by making relevant studies of high quality available to the profession at reasonable cost.

The Rcn is very happy indeed to publish this series of research reports. The projects were chosen by the individual research worker and the findings are those of the researcher and relate to the particular subject in the situation in which it was studied. The Rcn, in accordance with its policy of promoting research awareness among members of the profession, commends this series for study but views expressed do not necessarily reflect Rcn policy.

British Library Cataloguing in Publication Data

Stapleton, Mary F.
Ward sisters.
1. Nurses—In-service training
I.Title
610'.73'0711   RT76

ISBN 0-902606-75-1

Published by
The Royal College of Nursing of the United Kingdom,
Henrietta Place, Cavendish Square, London, W1M 0AB.

Printed by the Whitefriars Press Ltd. Tonbridge

Contents

List of Figures

List of Tables in the Text

Preface

At a school of nursing ceremony of award of certificates the presenter is often a senior member of the profession who is apt to take the opportunity of a short address to tell those newly qualified that their nursing education is only just beginning. This truth could be enlarged to point out that the need to assimilate new knowledge remains throughout a nurse's career, for health care is always in a state of change and development. Further, that the qualified nurse is personally responsible for keeping his or her own knowledge up-to-date. Society expects nothing less of a professional person.

But how realistic is this expectation in today's world?

At least two factors mitigate against it. One is certainly the pace and multiplicity of developments in health care itself and influences upon it from rapid advances in science and technology. Indeed, nurses themselves are now contributing to advancement of the body of knowledge in many aspects of health care by undertaking research, all of which needs to be known to every trained nurse if decisions and actions are to be based on the best available information.

The second factor is connected with the current nature of the nursing workforce. While still predominantly a female occupation, the single woman has been largely replaced by the married woman, often with a young family or teenage children. Moreover, with the rise in the number of people surviving into old age, many nurses now have an elderly relative dependent upon them for care. The likelihood of home commitments, plus the undoubted increasing pressure of work when on duty, therefore, begs the question—how can the qualified nurse be helped to maintain educational up-dating?

Mary Stapleton set herself the task of finding out, using one health authority region to explore the issues in depth. Publication of her research, for which she was awarded a Master's Degree by the University of Surrey, should be welcomed by every qualified nurse and midwife whether in clinical practice, management or post-basic education, since it concerns the vital matter of upholding professional standards in today's world.

DOREEN NORTON, OBE, MSc. (Soc), SRN, FRCN.
formerly Nursing Research Liaison Officer,
South West Thames Regional Health Authority

Acknowledgements

I wish to thank all the nurses who helped in this research, either by contributing to its development or by returning completed questionnaires and the nurse managers who gave access to the Districts in which the research was undertaken. I also wish to thank Dr. C. Bagley and Dr. A. Tropp who supervised the project, the DHSS which provided funds and librarians everywhere, especially Sue Merriott. Thanks are also due to Worthing Health District and to Karen Poulton who gave endless encouragement.

Introduction

The research was undertaken to ascertain the views of trained nurses on the need for ongoing professional education and the availability of such education as perceived by nurses in one health region. The main tool used was a questionnaire developed for the research, for which two ordinal scales were devised. Some questions were dichotomous, some open-ended and two questions contained four-point scales.

The sample of 284 nurses contained respondents of two grades, charge nurses and nursing officers; and from two divisions, general nurses and midwives. These nurses were from forty-five hospitals which were situated in urban and rural areas. The hospital size varied from less than 50 beds to more than 200 beds.

The results indicated that charge nurses in the general divisions exhibited low levels of satisfaction with the facilities for ongoing education provided for them. Midwives, who have statutory 'refresher' courses were more satisfied than general nurses. Nursing officers in the general divisions were more satisfied than charge nurses. Respondents were aware of facilities for post-basic specialist training and realistic in their perceptions of other facilities.

This report is based on a thesis submitted for a Master of Philosphy degree. The review of the literature which introduces the study describes the development of nursing as we know it and touches on the theory associated with role development. The roles of interest in this research are identified in the preceding paragraphs.

A social survey approach was made using as the primary tool a questionnaire and enhancing the data collected with information from semi-structured interviews with some of the respondents. The different methods of analysis used for different types of data are described and conclusions are drawn from the information collected. These conclusions are discussed in the final Chapter. The Tables in which the data are presented are not available in this report. These may be found in the thesis (Stapleton 82).

CHAPTER 1

Developments in Nursing

1.1 As It Was In The Beginning

The nursing service, as we accept it today, derives from the vision of Florence Nightingale. Funds subscribed by the nation after the Crimean War, with its dramas of Scutari, enabled her to finance a training school at St. Thomas' Hospital in 1860, which influenced nurse training throughout the country. However, Abel-Smith (1977) reminds us that King's College Hospital operated a training school for nurses by 1856, and Cartwright (1977) noted the influence on Miss Nightingale of the reforms to nursing practice instituted by Sister Mary Jones, of the Sisterhood of St. John the Evangelist in 1848. Cartwright also noted the difficulties that the Nightingale system engendered during its initial stages when what he calls a 'cadre of educated women' were being encouraged to spread the gospel of high standards of care of the sick to be undertaken by nurses who were trained in these skills. He describes the movement as being in the control of women

"... who all too often condescended to their work, regarded themselves as 'gifted' to clear up the mess made by the ignorant male and treated their colleagues, administrators and medical staff alike, as underlings whose sole duty lay in obeying their commands."

There is documented evidence of friction between the new nurses and the hospital establishments of the time. Abel-Smith (1977) cited Miss Burt's problems at Guy's Hospital. South's (1857) pamphlet in defence of the existing nursing service at St. Thomas' Hospital also indicated difficulties. Mr. South differentiated between the nurses and the sisters and his reference to the treatment of older sisters by medical staff as being similar to the way they treated 'old superior family servants' would be recognised by Katz (1969). He considered that the attitude of present day medical staff (in America) to nurses is reminiscent of the old caste system operating in the southern states of America, where whites despised negroes in general but could hold individual negroes in fond regard and treat them kindly.

Mr. South did not view 'nurses' as a general term for an occupation which could produce people with increased expertise in certain skills, such as administrative skills, as evidenced by the existence of ward sisters and matrons and White (1975) contended that he is 'patronising

11

and condescending' towards nurses which indicates agreement with Katz. White also noted that the present confusion that surrounds the functions of the trained nurse in the ward is an old problem since ward sisters (the present day charge nurses) have always been more concerned with the organisation of care than the giving of such care themselves. Pembrey (1978) suggested that charge nurses are now abdicating their responsibility for the organisation of care and that this lack of role differential results in a reduction in the standards of nursing which reaches patients since the ability to observe and supervise is lost, if the charge nurse role does not incorporate them in practice.

Miss Nightingale's "Missionaries" spread to voluntary hospitals in England and further afield. This new organisation of nursing had matrons who were trained nurses and who were responsible for all aspects of the nursing service offered (Seymer, 1956). Trained nurses of 'Sister' grade were in charge of wards in which nursing care was undertaken by nursing probationers whose duties included much which was of a housekeeping nature, a practice continued almost to the present day. Such activities enabled sisters to control the cleanliness of the ward and thus to develop a satisfactory environment in which patients' recovery could take place. The effect of lack of control over domestic cleanliness has been noted by Graham (1980) when he stated in the nursing press that nurses should have restored to them full authority over ancillary staff working in their area, because the result of lack of control has been "... a great decline in standards of hygiene" and he goes on to say that "... any casual inspection of hospital corridors and even ward areas will bear this out."

In developing the new nursing, Miss Nightingale's ladies frequently needed the backing of their powerful mentor. It is evident that some of the leaders of the medical world also supported the new nursing development since without this approval the process of nurse training would never have had access to hospitals in which to operate. Since the new scientific approach to medical care developed (Foucault, 1973) medical staff needed a reliable, obedient, intelligent helper to enable them to enact this new role. It was also true that doctors had very little idea of what is now and what then was Miss Nightingale's concept of nursing, (South, 1857; Nightingale, 1970). That there was a need for what can now be designated as nursing can be identified by the rapidity with which the principle of nurse training swept the country. Between 1860, when the Nightingale School opened, and 1892 voluntary hospitals had accepted the role of the trained nurse and had matrons who were themselves nurses and in charge of nurses (Abel-Smith, 1977). The year 1881 saw the appointment of Miss Manson to St. Bartholomew's Hospital. In 1887, Miss Manson became Mrs. Bedford Fenwick and she was thereafter active in nursing politics. Hector (1973) identifies some of the changes which occurred in nursing during

Miss Manson's career; for example, the renown of the training school, the increased time required for training and the improvement in working conditions.

Mrs. Bedford Fenwick left active nursing when she married but gave a lifetime of effort towards the development of nursing as a profession. Hector (1973) also illustrated the conditions of patients recovering from surgery by quoting a sister of that period describing her own training. She mentioned three methods of healing; first intention, granulation and suppuration of which she saw only suppuration, which indicates the activities which occupied nurses of the period.

It is interesting that the methods chosen to spread the gospel of nursing across the country is questioned by both White (1975) and Cartwright (1977) who suggested that the youth and inexperience of the ladies involved may have resulted in lack of subtlety in the approach they used and that this may have generated unnecessary opposition. However, White also noted that in the municipal hospitals, nurses used less confrontation because their organisation was such that they had no authority except that which the medical officer allowed them and they became skilled at introducing new practices by stealth, which enabled withdrawal to take place if the time for such changes seemed inopportune. It is, however, doubtful if such methods really proved their worth since Baly (1973) tells us that nursing in most United Kingdom non-teaching hospitals was not involved in decision making or planning until the implementation of the new management structure for nurses following the Report of the Committee on Senior Nursing Staff Structure (1966) commonly called the Salmon Report.

1.2 Pathways To Today

This century has generated a steady stream of investigations into nursing. The years up to 1919 were punctuated by the battles associated with the pros and cons of registration. Mrs. Bedford Fenwick led the pro registration faction and after Florence Nightingale's death in 1910 the battle against registration was spearheaded by Miss Luckes, the Matron of The London Hospital. Hector (1973) tells us of Miss Luckes' view of nurses in relation to the ability of an ordinary woman to work a 14 hour day every day of the week:

> "I do not think a nurse is an ordinary woman or she would not have chosen work which taxes her feelings and energies, mental and physical, so much."

Hector also describes Miss Luckes as not wishing to degrade the high art of nursing to the status of a mere profession.

Bills were brought before Parliament year after year between 1904 and 1914 and were rejected. The First World War, however, changed

13

attitudes. With the possibility of the enfranchisement of women the matter became of more importance to politicians and in 1919 Dr. Addison, the first Minister for Health, introduced a Bill which was passed in December. Doctors, of course, had been heavily involved in the controversy, both supporting and deploring registration (Bendall and Raybould, 1969). The Nurses' Act, then, enabled the formation of the General Nursing Council for England and Wales. This body was responsible for the registration of nurses and for the development of a training syllabus. The period of turbulence for nurses was by no means over, since battles over the registration of existing nurses and the acceptance of hospitals as training schools became central issues. However, by 1923 the General Nursing Council produced a format for examinations. Preliminary examination papers were comprised of:

a. Two of one and half hours each to include anatomy, physiology, hygiene, nursing
b. 20 minutes oral, and
c. 30 minutes practical examination

Final examination papers included:

a. medicine, surgery, gynaecology, medical, surgical and general nursing
b. 20 minutes oral, and
c. 35 minutes practical examination

This study, concentrating as it does upon the educational needs of charge nurses in the field of general nursing, has not pursued the difficulties associated with registration for the supplementary registers. The area is a fascinating one and is worthy of further study but it is peripheral to the present research. Midwives also, having achieved recognition by the opening of the midwives register in 1902, are worthy of more investigation than is offered here, and further information on the development of the midwifery service is to be found in Donnison's (1977) recently published history. All of the midwives in this study were registered general nurses with the added qualification of State Certification in midwifery. In this research midwives are of interest as a specialist group of nurses, of similar grades to general nurses, who already have a statutory obligation to attend updating programmes of five days duration every five years. These programmes, approved by the Central Midwives Board, are available at several centres throughout England and Wales. Midwives may not practise if this obligation is not fulfilled.

In 1932, the Lancet Commission on Nursing published a report. The terms of reference of this commission required them to offer suggestions for making nursing more attractive to women suited to the work and 'suited' seemed to mean well educated. The existence of the

14

Commission indicated that, with the continued expansion of health services and the sophistication of medicine, the demand for nurses outstripped the supply. Baly (1973) noted that the paucity of other career opportunities influenced many of the educated women who actually entered nursing, rather than the standards required of recruits. The Lancet Commission's recommendations included:

A reduction in the hours worked—not more than 10 hours daily, excluding time off.

Advance notice of duty patterns—to enable the planning of social activities.

Less rigid regulations regarding the Nurses' Homes.

Improvements in sisters' salaries with a £10 annual payment to recognise ward teaching.

In addition, the Commission commented upon the lack of assertiveness of ward sisters regarding living conditions. The Commission found that these women resented, not the infringement of their freedom, but the lack of differentiation in these infringements between themselves and nurses in training.

This Commission contained only two nurse members out of a complement of 12. This perhaps illustrates the views of the society of the time and indicates the paternalistic attitude of the medical profession towards nursing. White's (1975) views on this have been noted and Bagley (1974) also argued that nursing as an occupation suffers both from society's view of women as subservient to men and nurses as subservient to doctors. Another recommendation of the Commission, that the preliminary examination be so structured that part could be undertaken before leaving school was a matter of considerable controversy for several years. In 1939 the interim report of the Interdepartmental Committee on Nursing Services, (commonly known as the Athlone Report) was still exercised by the lack of opportunity available to nurses to plan their social lives and recommended higher rates of pay, longer holidays and no more than a 96 hour fortnight. It was the Athlone Report which recommended the acknowledgement of a grade of nurse lower than the State Registered Nurse, to take account of the many women of varying amounts of experience and little or no training who were already working in hospitals and that a roll should be kept of these nurses.

In the years before the 1919 Nurses' Act a Nurses' Association had been organised, one of several associations founded by Mrs. Bedford Fenwick and in 1916 the College of Nursing Ltd came into existence. It is this College which later became the Royal College of Nursing. From its inception the College was concerned with the better training of nurses and the advancement of nursing as a profession. By 1918 its Department of Education was involved in the development of tutor courses and later in courses for nurses involved in other work. Health

15

visitors were also offered training. This department, later to be the Division of Nursing Education (and in 1970 the Institute of Advanced Nursing Education) was also concerned in the development of the Diploma in Nursing Studies offered by the University of London. The Education Department of the College in Birmingham produces programmes, approved by the Joint Board of Clinical Nursing Studies, of specialist interest. There are also short programmes on the application of research to nursing activities.

It was the Royal College of Nursing which in 1942 commissioned the Nursing Reconstruction Committee, under the Chairmanship of Lord Horder (the Report of which was published in 1943) to consider the implementation of the Athlone Committee's Interim Report and the 1943 Nurses' Act enabled the General Nursing Council to enrol those nurses recommended by the Athlone Committee and later to develop training for this grade of nurse, first recognised as the enrolled assistant nurse and later as the State Enrolled Nurse.

These developments preceded the National Health Service Act of 1946 but in the years that followed the paradox that existed in nursing, that it was both monolithic and in a constant state of ferment, continued. Report followed report:

> The Recruitment and Training of Nurses (Ministry of Health, Department of Health for Scotland, Ministry of Labour and National Service, 1947)
> The Work of Nurses in Hospital Wards (Nuffield Provincial Hospitals Trust, 1953)
> Reform of Nursing Education (Royal College of Nursing, 1964)
> The Committee on Senior Nursing Staff Structure (Ministry of Health, Scottish Home and Health Department, 1966)
> The Report of the Committee on Nursing (Department of Health and Social Security, Scottish Home and Health Department and Welsh Office, 1972)
> The Report of the Royal Commission on the Health Services (Department of Health and Social Security, 1979 (with a chapter on nurses and midwives)

In examining the above list, one is interested in those reports which generated new thinking and whether this thinking resulted in action. The Athlone Report saw many of its recommendations implemented. The Wood Report of 1947 which recommended far reaching changes in the status of nurse learners, precipitated little action and much controversy. The Work of Nurses in Hospital Wards (by H. Goddard) resulted in the introduction of new terminology which, taken out of its context resulted, in McFarlane's (1976) view, in the debasement of actions directly related to patient care—'technical' equalled highly skilled and 'basic' equalled low skilled and the effects of this interpretation are still influencing nursing attitudes. A Reform of

16

Nursing Education, the Platt Report of 1964, despite the efforts of the Royal College of Nursing resulted in little action. The Salmon Report, on the other hand, was implemented in its entirety over a period of very few years, while the Report of the Committee on Nursing (the Briggs Report of 1972) with major recommendation of a change in the structure of the organisation of nurse training has taken seven years to reach the statute books. Another reorganisation of the Health Services has already followed the Report of the Royal Commission on the Health Sevices. It is too early to say what other changes will follow.

Mackenzie (1979) considering the differing speeds in relation to action following the Salmon and Briggs' Reports has this to say about the Salmon Report:

"... it is much more plausible to see this as a scheme attractive to lay administrators at each level, from the Treasury, through the Ministries, down through the hierarchy of lay administrators and finance officers. It purported to clarify a very confused situation."

Mackenzie also suggested that there was a vested interest among technicians of work study and organisation and methods, who had already done much work and recognised the need for a great deal more if the report were implemented. Baly (1973), however, regarded the report of the Prices and Incomes Board (1968) as the critical operating factor. Mackenzie considered that nurses had nothing to lose from the new structure and that nurse administrators had much to gain and that these factors combined with the others to make implementation something to be encouraged. What Mackenzie saw as available to nurses through the Salmon pattern of organisation was an improved career structure and improved financial conditions. The question of an improved career structure for nurses is discussed later in this report when data collected at interviews with Charge Nurses and Nursing Officers are presented.

The effect of the Salmon structure upon nursing is also discussed later in Chapter 2 in relation to nursing officers but it is useful to discuss the report itself since the results of its implementation were so far reaching. Davies (1977) commenting on the changes recommended by the Salmon Report (1966) argued that these changes were well suited to what she identified as a latent occupational strategy related to nursing. As in Miss Nightingale's day, Davies posited, nurses moved by improving their position in the power structure by means of management control and it was the loss of status at this level, which had been operating since the inception of the National Health Service which eroded the power and status of nurses. The attempts of the Royal College of Nursing to interest the government in the care/prevention aspect of nursing had foundered on the power struggles going on elsewhere. Cartwright (1977) also suggested such manipulations although he does not view these behaviours as part of an overall strategy, latent or otherwise.

In the following Chapters the role of the nurse is examined in the light of some existing theories. Nurses are part of the general social structure and changes in society have implications for nurses. The role of the nurse is recognised as being primarily concerned with the helping, nurturing aspects of patient care, the need to offer succour to the sick being the principal component of the role. The nurse, however, is also an employee, and is part of a hierarchical structure. She/he must not only deliver care to patients but may be concerned with the organisation of such care, and with the mobilisation of resources to make care possible. In a hierarchical structure this may require considerable skills in the art of assessment and negotiation. In addition to the nursing heirarchy other structures exist within the organisation of a hospital. Other disciplines with aims similar to those of nurses but with different priorities compete for resources of time, material and manpower. Different statuses exert differing degrees of power and the nurse directly involved in the delivery of patient care must enable the patient to have access to the services offered by, for example, catering departments, medical practitioners, investigative facilities and treatment personnel, in addition to the delivery of nursing services. Figure 1 shows the roles which interact with the charge nurse and give some indication of the multiplicity of demands made upon the holder of such a role.

1.3 Role Development

It is necessary, before discussing the educational needs of nurses, to define nursing and the nurse. Melia (1979) suggested that, for a sociological perspective, an examination of 'role' is crucial to the understanding of function. To this end an attempt has been made to discuss some theories associated with role in general terms and to consider the difficulties associated with changes in long established roles or the introduction of new roles in a hospital environment, which as Georgopoulas and Mann (1972) indicated, is complex, since, as an organisation it demands rules but these cannot cover all the eventualities generated by patients who are not necessarily passive and make their own demands upon staff.

Gross, Mason and MacEachern (1958) defined 'role' as a set of expectations—a set of evaluative standards applied to an incumbant of a particular position. Smith (1976) conceptualised role in terms of activity and defined it as a patterned sequence of learned actions performed by an individual in society. He reminded us that roles can be reciprocal for example, parent—child, husband—wife, nurse—patient and Banton (1965) classified role in terms of differentiation. Thus, he

18

FIGURE 1
Ward Sister Service Co-ordination Chart
(From the Report on the Feasibility of Achieving Nursing Economies and
Increased Efficiency in Hospital and Community Nursing Services).

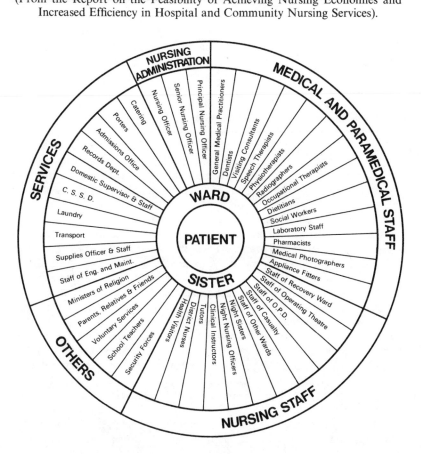

said, sex may affect the way people respond to an individual, as may
occupation, with its implication of class difference but leisure roles, for
example, may have little effect outside the area in which they are
enacted. Smith (1976) described roles which articulate with each other
as a role set. In hospital an example of the role set of the charge nurse
could contain patient, relative, doctor, student nurse, housekeeper,
porter, nursing officer (see Figure 1). Banton (1965) further discussed
signs in terms of uniforms, badges etc. and this is important in
hospitals where many of the role differentiations are indicated by
uniform change.

Johnson and Martin (1958) analysed the nurse role in relation to that of the doctor in terms of the degree of instrumental and expressive elements they both contain.

TABLE 1
Comparison of Doctor Nurse Functions

Functions	Doctor	Nurse
Instrumental	Primary	Secondary
Expressive	Secondary	Primary

Identifying the instrumental aspects of the social systems devised by the doctor—patient—nurse triad, they saw the medical functions as striving, by means of investigation, diagnosis and the prescription of treatment, directly towards the goal of patient recovery. The nurse, they described as being more involved in the tension reducing aspects; presenting the medical view to the patient and presenting the patient view to all significant others. This presentation of role implicitly accepts Parson's (1972) view of the patient's voluntarily relinquishing certain responsibilities by the very act of becoming a patient, therefore, accepting temporarily the dependent role in the triadical relationship, which is legitimised by the "ill" label. It is true that Illich (1976) and Kennedy (1980) disputed this legitimacy, making a plea for the demystification of medicine which would allow the patient to participate in decision making; but society gives at least tacit acceptance of it and the present interaction between nurse, patient and doctor acknowledges this acceptance. Thus nursing is seen, even when technical procedures are involved, as directed by the nurse to show caring, comforting attitudes and in producing this environment the nurse is contributing the nursing element of the patient's recovery. Maclean (1974) reinforced this viewpoint when she identified traditional designations of nurse—sister—matron and related them to the nurturing aspects of the nursing role. Banton (1965) in discussing roles, noted also their competitive aspects and stated that occupants of roles can develop protective perceptions of other roles with which they interact. For example, an achieving role may be seen by non-achievers as conceited and the non-achievers may be seen by achievers as jealous. Such a situation may complicate the development of new roles and in nursing, the nursing officer/charge nurse interaction may be affected in this way.

Areas of conflict may exist in nursing, for example, this could occur when being a mother prevents the enactment of the charge nurse role to the satisfaction of the role occupant, or conflicts which can exist if, for example, the charge nurse's (subordinate) view of the nursing officer role is different from the view held by senior nursing officers (superordinates). Such lack of congruence could give rise to role tensions for the nursing officer. This lack of congruence, however, does not necessarily lead to conflict. Parsons (1957) considered that new thinking may occur as a result and stimulate the development of roles. Out of conflict also, strategies may occur which allow the role to change. However, in the absence of coping mechanisms, such conflict may be the source of high levels of anxiety. In hospitals this anxiety has been noted by Revans (1964), Menzies (1960) and Cartwright (1964).

The impact that specialisation has upon key roles has been described by Southall (1959) who indicated that a proliferation of such specialist roles must diminish the content of the original role. Thus, in hospitals, the advent of the specialist roles of dietitians, physiotherapists, radiographers and housekeepers has reduced the breadth of the nurse role. This reduction in breadth should allow the development in depth of the "caring", "expressive" aspects of the role. However, as Senior (1978) suggested, the nurse role is still implicitly, if not explicitly, involved with most of the other aspects. Dietary advice may not always be available but the patient must be fed. Housekeepers and therapists, in the main, keep office hours but routine needs make demands upon the nurse throughout the 24 hours. The expressive aspects of the role cannot be switched on and off since, if the patient perceives that caring, comforting interactions are denied in one situation they may no longer respond in another more "appropriate" interaction. This may prevent the nurse role being fully operational at any level. The response of the nurse to patient needs may be on an expressive affective level but demonstrated at an operational level, such as, the giving of food or drink and so efforts to constrain nursing to certain limited aspects of patient care are thwarted by the nurturing aspects of nursing which cannot function on an intermittent basis. It is, therefore, arguable that the reduction in the breadth of the nurse role is more apparent than real. In depth, the role is continuing to develop, since the rapid increase in knowledge in the biological sciences, together with the expansion of the behavioural sciences, (Chapman, 1977 and Staunton, 1979) has created an environment which has contributed to societal change. This makes it necessary to examine the professional educational inputs available to trained nurses and to determine what they themselves recognise as educational needs in this dynamic situation.

To nurse implies the existence of patients and people become patients by means of their relationship with doctors. These roles, those of patient, doctor, nurse interact with one another within the hospital setting. However, differences exist. Patient is differentiated by means of the acceptance of a state of dependency (Smith, 1976) and Parsons (1972) stated that the sick person is allowed exemption from the performance of normal social role obligations and exemption from responsibility for his own state. The doctor copes with the patient's need by means of investigation, diagnosis and the prescription of treatment. The nurse undertakes delivery of the prescribed treatment and generates nursing care to meet the levels of dependence exhibited by the patient. This includes observation and recording of various signs and symptoms. The interaction between the roles of nurse and doctor makes role differentiation more difficult.

Gilbertson, (1977) writing of the confused role of the ward sister in New Zealand, stated that role ambiguity and misunderstanding are often functions of unclear training objectives and varying expectations of those who interact with such particular roles. He argued that text book definitions of the role are not tested by research and posited a need for such research within a framework of applied role theory as a basis for understanding the complexities of the role as it is undertaken, since, he stated, it is clearly understood that:

"... the crucial source of initiation to achieve patient care in a total sense must come from the ward sister."

Research in this country relating to the charge nurse role is concerned with certain limited although important aspects of the role, for example, Pembrey (1978) examined the management component of the role and Fretwell (1980) and Ogier (1979) the teaching component. How these components are integrated into the whole has not yet been adequately examined.

CHAPTER 2

Different Grades of Nurses

2.1 The State Registered Nurse

Roper (1976) defined nursing in these terms:

> "Within the context of a health care system and in a variety of combinations, nursing is helping a person towards his personal independent pole of the continuum of each Activity of Daily Living: helping him to remain there, helping him to cope with any movement towards the dependent pole or poles; in some instances encouraging him to move towards the dependent pole or poles; and because man is finite, helping him to die with dignity."

The nurses' interpretation of the role they are intending to enact allows them to identify the skills they will need to undertake the role. It also enables the charge nurse to be seen within this framework as a co-ordinator, deliverer and teacher of nursing care. The definition encompasses the nurse's complementary relationship with the doctor's activities of diagnosis of disease and prescription of treatment and enables the nurses to identify the nursing component of care. Roper considered that nursing does not benefit from the current disease labels used to identify the patient's health since nursing is concerned with the patient's condition and not his disease label—a point also made by the Scottish National Nursing and Midwifery Consultative Committee (1976).

Henderson (1978) asked, "Is there a universal concept of nursing?" She goes on to state that before answering the question she must reconstruct it to enable her to identify for whom the concept is required; if it is for the public at large, for other health workers, or for nurses themselves. Henderson posits that the elements common to all these groups might be identified as a universal concept of nursing. However, in 1968, Henderson defined nursing for the International Council of Nurses in these terms:

> "The unique function of the nurse is to assist the individual sick or well in the performance of those activities contributing to health or its recovery which he would perform unaided if he had the necessary will or knowledge, and to do this in such a way as to help him to independence as rapidly as possible."

This concept of nursing can be related to Roper's identification of the nurse as helper in the activities of daily living.

McFarlane (1976) referred to the nurse as a "continuity man" both as a giver of care and as a co-ordinator of care, acting as a surrogate for doctor, patient or relative in turn and having a major professional contribution to make, marked by the nature of the acts she performs. She stressed the helping, assisting, serving nature of the nursing role and suggested that this dimension, which Henderson (1978) also stressed, is in danger of playing a subsidiary part and being relegated to the "unskilled" to undertake, these tasks being considered unworthy of the technicians role that nurses are in danger of assuming. Austen (1976) also made this point when she discussed the reduction in status of the work undertaken in the home, relating it to the advance of technology debasing tasks and thus reducing the status of those undertaking these tasks. Austen was describing the work of women in the home. In nursing, increasing technology surrounding the patient is causing the essential care tasks to lose status and with the reduction in the status of the tasks, reduction in the status of those undertaking these tasks—nurses. The extension of the role to enable nurses to undertake high status procedures such as those which have become routine for doctors, has always been part of the pattern of development in nursing but it is only now that the quantity of such tasks is challenging nursing in its essentials, since only recently has technology developed its present multiplicity of demands. For example, the present tendency for nurses to undertake the intravenous administration of drugs has resulted in an increase in prescriptions for the delivery of medication in this way. Constraints previously operating, that doctors themselves administered drugs by this route, presumably acted as a control on this type of prescription. The removal of this constraint has resulted in considerable increase in this type of nursing activity. Since the nurse involved must be a trained nurse and the only trained nurse available is often the charge nurse, the additional time consumed by drug administration has a concomitant effect upon the charge nurse's ability to supervise and co-ordinate care or to teach.

The proposal made by McFarlane (1976) for the development of the role of the nurse rather than for its extension, stems from her definition of "development", which she related to the helping, assisting, aspects of nursing and "extension", which she defined as moving away from the patient towards medically derived tasks. Both Roper (1976) and Hunter (1971) touched on the process of role development, when they commented on the inadequacy of the medical model as a basis for professional development in nursing. Hunter considered that nursing could and should encompass both the technical tasks abdicated by the doctor and the increasing theory now becoming available to nursing to enable nurses to develop social and relational skills. MacGuire (1964) and Dodd (1973), however, found that nurses were reluctant to

24

acknowledge the possibility of acquiring such skills, which they considered to be part of the personality and, therefore, there or not there; not skills which could be learned. That nurses of learner status were in the process of socialising into nursing and thus learning to relate to patients and other workers, was not identified by nurses in Dodd's study as being indicative of an ability to acquire skills of this kind. Quenzer (1974) also noted that nurses seem unaware that such interpersonal skills contributed to a therapeutic environment for the patient. Pepper (1977) and Ogier (1979) indicated that charge nurses would benefit from further training in interpersonal skills, suggesting that charge nurses recognised that they lacked such training.

Saunders (1954) discussing the ambiguous status of the nurse, noted that she is expected to have extensive knowledge, master complicated skills and carry heavy responsibilities, but that society offers relatively low rewards for this. Chapman (1977) made something of the same point when she commented on the medical view of the nursing role and considered that, although doctors want an intelligent observer and a nurse capable of carrying out complicated technical procedures, they do not want a "colleague". They see the emergence of nurses from degree courses as a threat to the medical monopoly of knowledge. She also considered that doctors see intelligence and the desire and ability to deliver nursing care to patients as mutually exclusive and thought that this view exacerbates the situation. Devine (1978) also identified this lack of role definition, noting that as subordinates, nurses are expected to render obedience to superiors and to conform to rules and regulations. At the same time as professionals they are being encouraged to consider themselves autonomous. Devine's study took place in Nova Scotia but charge nurses in this country might well identify with the findings. It is useful to compare Devine's view of the situation with the somewhat more rarified definition of nursing offered by Schlotfeldt (1965). Here the nursing role is seen in terms of "meeting the patient's needs" by means of assessment of the interpersonal and environment climate so that it can be made therapeutic. The nurse is seen as working with the doctor as a true professional and negotiating with the doctor on the basis of patient need, as to who should assume responsibility for a particular aspect of the therapeutic regimen at any point in time. In Devine's study there is little evidence that doctors pay any more than lip service to the concept of the nurse as a professional nor was there any evidence that doctors saw nurses as partners in a decision making process, despite the episodic nature of medical care which Hyderbrand (1973) commented upon. Bendall (1973) saw the lack of role definition in nursing as leading to a process of status reduction and cited three measures used by nurses to offset this:

1. The tendency to increase the academic qualifications required of entrants, is one method, used as a general attempt to lever up the

"floor" upon which nursing is based. There is no research evidence, Bendall stated, upon which to consider an appropriate level of educational qualifications for entrants to nursing but professionalisation suggests academic standards.

2. Tutors have made their own bid for status enhancement by supporting the development of teachers, lecturers and professors of nursing.

3. The Salmon structure brought status enhancement to nursing managers.

However, both teachers and managers suffer professional status deprivation in that they have moved away from the direct delivery of patient care and in this situation Bendall saw a particular threat to status security. Grosvenor (1978) however, considered that this is a feature among practice disciplines generally not only among nurses and that practitioners, secure in the knowledge that they are providing a service for other people which would be missed immediately were it withdrawn, have a clear justification for their existence. Managers, Grosvenor agreed, lack this clear definition of usefulness and consequently lean more heavily on other status supports. MacKenzie (1979) suggested that this explains the pressure of nurses in management roles for the development of a rational management structure.

The state of organising nursing care, instead of directly delivering patient care, has been noted by Corwin (1961) as being associated with role ambiguity in nursing, in the United States. Corwin found that well defined role conception is positively associated with personal self assurance and that staff, who when deprived of a clear conception of their role, could distance themselves from such a threat to self, by moving away from the ambiguous role. Dodd (1973) identified the problem at another level. She recognised that tutors teaching an "ideal" type of nursing which is not operational in the real world, place an intolerable burden upon the nurse practitioner who has to adopt strategies of avoidance to cope with the situation and in doing so suffers further status threat. If technology has debased the nurturing aspects of nursing as Austen (1977) and Schulman (1972) suggested and if such debasement has resulted in loss of status and status reduction has created a loss of power, it can be deduced that lack of power at charge nurse level can affect the delivery of patient care. It is interesting that Merton (1960) acknowledged the need for nurses to seek professional status. He accepted their legitimising of this need within a framework of the possession of expertise which is exercised. Professional status carries with it the social accolade of autonomy and as Merton stated, autonomy is related to self-respect.

"In our society, as in many other societies, people find this measure of autonomy rewarding. They take satisfaction in knowing that it is they, not

26

others who decide what they are to do in a particular field of operation, how it is to be done and by whom it is to be done. Autonomy and its correlate, self-respect, are just as real rewards for human beings as money income, with all that that income makes possible. Were it not, many members of many professions would drift, in even larger numbers than they do now, into occupations where they receive more income but less respect. It is this fact, of course, that periodically leads to the economic exploitation of certain professions."

Austen (1977) also recognised that nurses seek their status rewards within the concept of professional development rather than hierarchical progress. It is in the field of nursing knowledge and its availability to practitioners that problems exist. The movement of nurses towards professional autonomy by means of managerialism noted by Davies (1976) is also considered by Johnstone (1978) who posited that this movement can lead to division between "enablers" and "carers", since the ritualistic deference behaviours which co-exist in nursing with the aspirations of professional striving may disguise these differences. Thus the nurse practitioner (in this research, the charge nurse) in her/his need to update knowledge relevant to nursing and to maintain status in nursing vis-a-vis patients, learners, colleagues and doctors may be forced to look towards the medical professional rather than to senior nurses if such nurses are not seen as a source of nursing knowledge of value to the nurse practitioner.

To clarify further the nursing roles under scrutiny, literature relating to the nurse in charge of wards was examined. In this country in the general field of nursing, the nurse in charge of a ward in a hospital traditionally was female and the designation "Sister" was used. Since the Second World War an increasing number of men have been accepted for training for the general register and this has meant that a greater number of wards have male nurses in charge. The designation charge nurse can be used for nurses of either sex and this is the term used in this report.

2.2 The Charge Nurse

Caseldine (1977) postulated that the charge nurse role demands so much of the nurse in terms of clinical knowledge and teaching ability, in addition to managerial skills, that it is no longer a realistic expectation. The growth of knowledge in today's world, allied to the loss of status which he associated with the introduction of the Nursing Officer role, leads to increasing difficulties for a charge nurse operating in the traditional manner. Caseldine maintained that it is now time to develop the role of the nurse in terms of the nursing consultant. Such a consultant nurse should be available to nursing practitioners in the ward situation who are heading teams of nursing staff giving direct care to patients. The administrative management, he considered,

27

should be under the control of nursing officers with clerks working in the wards, relieving nurses of administrative detail and thus truly enabling such nurses personally to operate as deliverers of care. This development moves far from the Goddard (1953) definition of the ward sister's (the present day charge nurse) functions. Goddard saw the charge nurse role as an amalgamation of three main components:

1. The supervision of nursing care and treatment.
2. The training of student nurses.
3. The co-ordination of services to the patient.

Subsumed under (1) is the interpretation of medical instruction and the delivery of medically prescribed treatment. Lelean (1973) noted that such interpretation can lead to difficulties when there is no written version of the medical order available. While drug prescriptions are always written, other medical instructions may not be and could, therefore, be interpreted by the charge nurse rather as a cue than a command. If the doctor views the instruction as a command rather than a cue the resultant action or lack of action may lead to variability in the understanding of treatment given. Wilson (1975) identified a difference in the doctor's perception of staff nurses' knowledge of the biological sciences and the amount of knowledge that such nurses actually possessed. Wilson was investigating the state of knowledge of staff nurses. However, no more knowledge is identified for the charge nurses since "appropriate" experience at staff nurse level is the principal criterion upon which charge nurse appointment are made. Thus the same degree of incongruence may exist between the doctor's perception of knowledge possessed and the actual knowledge possessed by the charge nurse. This may well influence the charge nurse's interpretation of the doctor's instruction and underlines the need for systematic updating to be available to charge nurses, more than 25% of whom, in the present research, trained 25 or more years ago.

Kerrane (1977), discussing the American nursing situation, as an indicator of the development of the nursing role in this country, noted the problems associated with the demands of highly technical nursing. These areas draw heavily on available nursing resources and give nursing care of a satisfactory standard. However, patients not requiring such technical services are nursed where they may have to be cared for by nursing aides who have practically no nursing skills at all. Kerrane posited that the adoption by nurses of tasks which doctors find less interesting than diagnosis and prescription, may well reduce the nurses' ability to maintain standards of nursing care, since time needed to care for patients will have been consumed by tasks delegated by doctors. Davies (1971) noted that nurses of charge nurse grade saw the delivery of treatment, ordered by medical staff, as the most important function of their role; an observation also made by Dodd

28

(1973). Davies (1971) interpreted this finding within the framework of Etzioni's (1969) definition of a semi-profession. However, the lack of control of work volume, which underpinned Davies' (1971) identification of this state, may well be based upon inadequate information. Pressures operating affect doctors and nurses alike and are societal rather than professional. The admission of patients in need of treatment is an uncontrollable variable in a national health service. This creates many problems in situations of inadequate resources whether the resources in short supply are human or financial. The nurse is primarily conscious of the needs of sick people who are labelled as patients when these patients are within the environs of the ward. Consultants, and by implication, their registrars, become responsible for patients when they hear of them, whether they are in the ward or not, so long as the patients are in the catchment area. The doctor is required to "treat" any who are in need of treatment if this need has been legitimised by referral from a general practitioner. That such patients may require only half-an-hour of the physician's time in treatment means that the doctor recognises his capacity to treat, but such half-an-hour of medical time may generate a demand for nursing care which spans all of the 24 hours. It is perhaps the separation rather than the affinity of goals which generates an area of conflict here.

The importance of involvement of 'nurse', whether charge or other grade in clinical interaction with patient, was noted by Williams (1969) Dodd (1973) and Pepper (1977). Williams indicated that for the charge nurse, the patient-centred aspects of the role were the aspects which were stressed. Administrators, ignoring the demands of such clinical elements, identified the charge nurse as a manager of services within the ward, thus intensifying the charge nurses' difficulties in influencing nursing outcomes. Anderson (1973) stated that doctors' expectations of the charge nurse were primarily that his instructions should be carried out and Dodd (1973) also found this. Dodd found, too, that charge nurses identified their authority in the ward as stemming from their ability to satisfy medical consultants rather than the nursing hierarchy. Bendall (1975) found that charge nurses could be doctor-centred rather than patient-centred and that this produced a particular type of ward environment which could be identified by the patient. This was also described by McGhee (1961), Revans (1962) and Cartwright (1964) who acknowledged the ward environment which is a direct effect of the variable "charge nurse" and Walker (1967) also mentioned this. Exchaquet (1967) noted another aspect of charge nurse control. She considered that charge nurses have moved from serving patients to serving all other departments within a hospital. She postulated that today's hospital nurses deliver upon demand, people, patients, material and time, so that such departments will not be inconvenienced. She contended that such developments produce efficiency at all levels except that of patient care. This again may relate to Austen's (1977) belief that increasing technology debases personal service.

Gilbertson (1977) posed two questions in relation to the role of charge nurse:

"1. What are the determinants of the ward sister role and what are resultant conflicts and ambiguities and their effect in terms of stress or other dysfunctions?
2. What are the factors resisting and facilitating the growth and development of a more professional health care team in various organisations?"

The organisation of the nursing service which followed the publication, in 1966, of the Report of the Committee on Senior Nursing Staff Structure (see Chapter 1, 1.2) was not research based. However, without adequate research, the rationalisation of nursing management resulted in the emergence of a new grade of nurse, the unit nursing officer, administratively responsible for groups of wards. This role impinges to some degree upon the functions of the charge nurse, and its development may well introduce further areas of difficulty for the nurse of charge nurse grade. The present research examines only one area of possible contribution to dysfunction in both the charge nurse role and the unit nursing officer role. This contribution is the availability or lack of educational inputs which may enable nurses of these grades to update nursing knowledge, and with this in view the following paragraphs look at the literature in order to establish understanding of the nursing officer role and to examine health service workers' (both nurses' and others') perception of the role.

2.3 The Nursing Officer

The rational system of management now existing in nursing derives from the implementation of the Report of the Committee on Senior Nursing Staff Structure (1966). In the report it is stated that nurses' views were found to have less status than the views of medical staff and hospital administrators in respect of meetings of governing bodies within the National Health Service. Subsequently, great emphasis was placed on the development of staff training in management skills and money was made available to fund such training. As a result of this report, a classical structure of management was imposed and nurses were graded from five to 10, dependent upon an increasing span of management responsibility. Salary was dependent upon grade. These grades are now described:

Grade 5   A State Registered Nurse who acts as assistant and
Staff Nurse   deputy to a charge nurse.

30

Grade 6 Ward Sister	Nurse in charge of a ward or department (for example, outpatient department). This designation is confusing when the person in charge is a man and the designation charge nurse is increasingly being used. (It is the designation charge nurse which is used throughout this report).
Grade 7 Unit Nursing Officer	A nurse in charge of a group of wards, (this could be a small hospital) or it could be a nurse in charge of a specialised unit, for example, a dialysis unit.
Grade 8 Senior Nursing Officer	A nurse in charge of a group of units, frequently a whole hospital.
Grade 9 Principal Nursing Officer	A nurse in charge of a main speciality, for example, general, midwifery, psychiatry. A single specialty could span several hospitals.
Grade 10 Chief Nursing Officer	A nurse in charge of all nursing services in a group of hospitals.

The reorganisation of the health services in Britain in 1974 resulted in community nursing services, which had previously been the responsibility of local authorities, coming under the control of the newly formed Health Districts. These Health Districts were to be monitored by Area Health Authorities, who allocated the funds distributed by Regional Health Authorities. Each of these authorities had their own teams of officers. District management teams now had a district nursing officer who was responsible for all nursing services within the district, both hospital and community based. Nursing divisions were developed. These were usually based on the main nursing specialties, which now included community divisions. The Salmon structure grades 9 and 10 became defunct and district nursing officers and divisional nursing officers were appointed. One other change in management for nurses which the implementation of the Salmon Report's recommendations brought about was the development of staff posts in nursing management for nurses with special expertise in certain key areas. These posts were often of senior nursing officer grade and, in the main, nurses offered skills in personnel, planning and infection control.

The totally new development which was introduced into the system was the role of the nursing officer.

31

The components of the nursing officer role identified by the Salmon Report (1966) were those of:

1. Nursing consultant.
2. Work programmer.
3. Staff controller.

Wilson-Barnett (1973) and Rowland (1976) examining the instrumental aspects of the nursing officer role found that 49% and 56% respectively of the nursing officer's working time was spent on administrative work and that a large part of the 37% of time which was spent in "patient directed activities" was taken up with "ward rounds". Both these researchers questioned the value of such "ward rounds" and suggested that other nursing activities might be undertaken to enable nurses of this grade to maintain their nursing competence. Ongley (1976) also writing of the way that nursing officers use their time, noted that 46% is spent on administration and all of these studies mentioned that little time was observed to be spent on "teaching" activities. Ongley also noted that the mean time spent on individual tasks was eight minutes and Rowland observed a mean time of four minutes. Ongley and Rowland both recorded that large amounts of nursing officer activities were unplanned. Clarke (1978) described the lack of identification of "planning" as a nursing activity and Lelean (1973), as discussed elsewhere in this report, noted the frequency of interruptions to which charge nurses were subjected. It may be that the ability to respond to needs as they arise is an essential attribute of the nursing officer function; or it may be an inheritance from the charge nurse role, where planning of activities was not recognised as a necessary skill. Smith (1977) examining the role of the nursing officer noted that participative observation produced a different emphasis on priority of activities from the replies elicited from the same group using questionnaires as a research tool. During observation nursing officers demonstrated their role as being mainly administrative, while written response indicated that the clinical aspects predominated. Smith speculated that observation produced "real world" information while the questionnaires indicated a psychological rationalisation and such answers could be considered to indicate an ideal and desirable state, a point also made by Hagburg (1970). In another study of the role of the nursing officer, however, Carr (1978) found that nursing officers' activities break down into: 20% of time spent on "teaching" with administrative and patient care activities using equal amounts of time, indicating that the role was well integrated into the service. Wall and Hespe (1972) suggested that dissatisfactions exist and Rowland (1976) and Wilson-Barnett (1973) noted that "communications could be a problem" and that "the hierarchy is too great". This could indicate a lack of delegation of responsibility which might be related to the lack of confidence in subordinates which Menzies (1960) described as part of the social defence system developed by nurses. Bagley (1977) delineated nurses of nursing officer grade as being in a state of anomic confusion. He identified them as being confronted with a confusing range of tasks coupled with a diversity of authority roles, where, he stated, who is accountable to whom has not emerged with any clarity nor are the occasions when they may act in the clinical capacity assigned to them very clear. Such a state of normlessness, he contended, results in great amounts of personal distress and unhappiness for the grades of staff affected.

The evidence, therefore, suggests that the varying facets of the nursing officer role do not articulate smoothly and that there is a concomitant degree of both intra and inter role conflict. Without the opportunity to develop greater expertise in nursing it is unrealistic to expect a nursing officer to operate in a clinical consultant role to a charge nurse who, even if she/he is in no better position regarding systematic inputs of knowledge, does have easier access to empirical knowledge relating to patient care. In addition, the demands of nurse managers senior to the nursing officer, may require performance which, in relation to available resources, could conflict with the nursing officers' perception of what is needed to provide adequate standards of patient care.

It is now necessary to identify how the present nursing structure evolved. Nursing was traditionally organised, since the development of the Nightingale School of Nursing at St. Thomas' Hospital, by means of a centralised control. The matron, with a varying number of assistants, organised the nursing service and was herself within the control of the senior administrative officer of the hospital, who might have been either a lay administrator or a medical superintendent. She might or might not meet with the governing body, (Hospital Management Committee or Board of Governors). The matron was very unlikely to have had a part in decision making (Salmon, 1966); being there by invitation and not of right.

The matron's assistants undertook such tasks as were delegated to them by her. These could vary from day to day. There was no continuity of relationships. In the main, such communication systems as operated between assistant matrons and ward staff and matron's office were erratic. The dissemination of information was liable to disruption, since such information could flow from matron to assistants and remain there; could flow from matron to ward staff, by-passing assistants; could move from ward staff to matron without informing assistants. One assistant matron could receive information without informing others, (Baly, 1973). Lines of authority were similarly muddled. Charismatic matrons existed and operated with flair and efficiency and systematic matrons introduced order and organisation but the service as a whole carried the legacy of its house-keeping antecedents and did not utilise any theory of management.

The development of a rational management structure for nurses had effects both within and surrounding the service. Bagley (1974) said of post-Salmon management in nursing that it brought to nursing an increase of power and it is this, he suggested, that irked medical consultants and others involved in traditional methods of hospital organisation. He noted how unbalanced the power statuses in hospitals were formerly and indentified the opportunity for nurses to take part in major decision making as being upsetting to all who had previously accepted the rightness of male dominance. Dewar (1966) reflected medical dissatisfactions with the structure when he cited the plight of the charge nurse, under the control of the nursing officer" . . . who will neither take doctors' instructions directly nor have the patients' confidence," indicating something of South's (1857) dissatisfaction with change in the structure of nursing management of an earlier age. Davies (1971) and Dodd (1973) noted that charge nurses themselves saw their authority as stemming directly from their relationship with medical staff and not from their relationship with senior nurses. Dewar (1978) made further comment on the nursing officer role indicating that he did not see this post as one which had an "enabling" function which would enhance the efficiency of the charge nurse. There is a tendency for medical staff to see all problems with nurses as stemming from the post Salmon structure. Thus Dewar also noted that patients prefer to ask junior nurses to perform small tasks for them rather than ask a charge nurse to do so. McGhee (1961) in her Scottish study also recorded this phenomenon, and Tagliacozzi and Mauksch (1972) described such patients as being reluctant to play the "consumer role" openly, considering that requests made of junior nursing staff allowed them to maintain a feeling that they remain in "credit" with the charge nurse. Tagliacozzi and Mauksch described this interaction in terms of "principles of social exchange" and suggested that patients act if the amount of service available were finite and this management of interaction helps them to feel an element of control over their own affairs. Rogers (1978) also viewed the change brought about by the development of the nursing officer role in much the same terms as did Mr. South in 1857. Rogers regretted the passing of ". . . the dowdy old ward sister" and the matron, both perhaps mother surrogate figures. Unlike Schulman (1972) who discussed this image of nursing, Rogers did not see the disappearance of such people as a response to generalised social pressures but as a result of organisational change. It is worth speculating that the use of the designation of unit matron rather than unit nursing officer might have generated less anxieties among medical staff if it were not for evidence that in 1966 matrons were viewed rather less favourably by doctors than subsequent recall indicates. Indeed Rudd (1973) indicated such attitudes when he suggested that something like a Salmon structure was needed to wrench power from the old type matrons who were, he stated, often autocrats. Rudd, however, viewed the nursing officer role as a means of enabling charge nurses to work more efficiently.

The Salmon Report (1966) recommended that there should be professional preparation and management training to enable staff to exhibit the appropriate degree of expertise to equip them to respond to the particular demands of the nursing officer role. The Salmon Report recommended that management preparation should be undertaken, in the first place, during periods of 12 weeks study. In practice this has been reduced to two weeks with varying numbers of days later allocated to modular inputs in a few topics. Bagley (1974) suggested that training in management for senior nurses should be the same as that which is necessary for membership of the Institute of Health Service Administrators, which is the equivalent of two years full time study. In nursing, clinical expertise is recognised as being needed in highly specialised areas and evidence of attendance at Joint Board of Clinical Nursing Studies courses is becoming obligatory for those in charge of units such as operating theatres, dialysing units etc. In less specialised areas such as medical or surgical units, appropriate experience is the requirement. As Argyris (1957) noted, however, it is not the experience but how people internalise aspects of the experience that is important. It is difficult to justify the nursing consultant component of the nursing officer role (attributed by the Salmon Report, 1966) if no evidence of an ongoing acquisition of knowledge relevant to nursing, and/or advance nursing education is required.

In this country, as has already been stated in Chapter 2, 2.3, the nursing contribution to the hospital as an organisation is by means of a staffing structure graded in Weberian terms (Chapman, 1976) from district nursing officers, in control of all nursing staff within a health district by means of divisional nursing officers, in control of divisions of nursing, to senior nursing officers, in charge of a group of units, through to nursing officers who are in charge of groups of wards and then to charge nurses who are in charge of single wards. Thus the charge nurse as exemplified by the Salmon Report is in a line relationship to the nursing officer for aspects of organisational policy and to the medical consultant for the delivery of medically prescribed treatment for patients. She/he also has autonomy in prescribing nursing care for individual patients. It is in this area of direct control of patient care that the current management organisation in nursing seems less than appropriate.

Georgopoulas and Mann (1972) described the hospital as an organisation which operates a human rather than a mechanical system needing day to day adjustments since the work cannot be standardised and variability makes assembly-line techniques inappropriate. Formalised rules cannot be devised to cover all eventualities. In addition to this they stated that patients are not necessarily passive and may make their own demands so that staff need flexibility to meet the human needs that illness generates. They went on to note the paradox which exists, as the hospital is also a highly formalised, quasi bureaucratic organisation. Like all task-orientated organisations it relies a great deal on formal policies and formal authority for controlling much of the behaviour and work relationships of its members. They observed distinct status differences among staff with sharp patterns of superordinate and subordinate grades.

The model below of the organisation of nursing is based on Weber's model of hierarchy and relates the concept of bureaucracy to the nurse management structure.

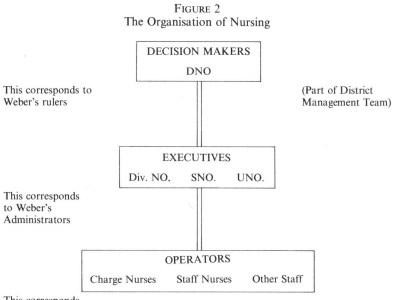

FIGURE 2
The Organisation of Nursing

DECISION MAKERS
DNO

This corresponds to
Weber's rulers

(Part of District
Management Team)

EXECUTIVES
Div. NO, SNO. UNO.

This corresponds
to Weber's
Administrators

OPERATORS
Charge Nurses   Staff Nurses   Other Staff

This corresponds
to Weber's subordinate
staff who comply with
instruction.

The model, however, ignores the complexities and paradoxes described by Georgopoulas and Mann and this over-simplification does not acknowledge the turbulence existing at ward level (Pembrey, 1978). This is demonstrated in a later model, (Figure 3) which reflects the unacknowledged dimensions which operate.

Within the human system described by Georgopoulas and Mann controlled by formal policies, hospitals are expected to provide care to patients at all times with the precision of a machine and with minimum error. This environment can promote problems for those who operate within it. Davies (1971) also stated this when she described the complexities of hospital organisation, noting that such organisations depend on people internalising the value system and being able to translate these values into behaviour. The high level of anxiety in which actions take place, generates, she said, the rules and procedures which are adopted and which provide prescribed responses to emergency decisions. These prescribed behaviours, said Davies, not only protect hospital employees from the effect of the high levels of anxiety, noted by other researchers (Menzies, 1960 and Revans, 1964) but also patients from the effect of decisions made under stress. Thus the model in Figure 2 demonstrates the concept of management applied to nursing following the implementation of the Salmon Report and it can be seen that little allowance has been made in organisational terms for the need for the flexibility recognised by Georgopoulas and Mann (1972). Woodward (1965) and Stewart (1970) noted that the type of activity undertaken within an organisation or the type of technology generating the activity in which an organisation is involved, determines the most appropriate type of management pattern for that organisation and this continues Burns and Stalker's (1961) work in identifying properties of organisations which were designated as "organistic" to describe dynamic, changeful, unstructured situations

FIGURE 3
Model Showing Complicated Lines of Authority Existing at Ward Level

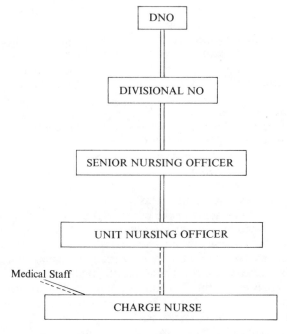

and "mechanistic" to describe the static, easily anticipated conditions existing in other situations. They designated the formal hierarchical management structure as appropriate to the "mechanistic" type of organisational system and suggested that a less rigid pattern is needed in fluid dynamic situations. Pembrey (1978) and Melia (1979) identified the ward in a hospital in the same terms as Georgopoulas and Mann (1972) and saw these areas as conforming to Burns and Stalker's (1961) "organistic" category and thus incapable of responding appropriately to the rigidity of the tightly structured line management visualised by the Salmon Report.

The model presented in Figure 3 indicates the increased organisational complexity existing at ward level. It can now be seen that the bureaucratic form is appropriate to the level of nursing officer. It thus reflects Weber's (1947) emphasis on the administrative function and attempts to illustrate the differences which exist at operational level.

The charge nurse is both directly responsible to the medical staff for the delivery of prescribed treatment and investigations (unbroken line) but not for how such care is delivered (broken line). Katz (1969) and Kelly (1966) noted this when they identified the fact that doctors give orders on certain aspects of patient care; but in the immediate delivery of services to the patient the charge nurse is in control. The charge nurse looks to the nursing officer for resources to undertake the delivery of nursing care to patients but is not responsible to the nursing officer for the delivery of such care to individual patients (broken and unbroken lines indicate these states).

The emphasis laid by the Salmon Report on the nursing officer as a clinical expert has a potential for complicating this situation with the risk of eroding the autonomy of the charge nurse within the boundaries of the ward, hitherto the nursing area which was undisputedly the area of clinical control of the charge nurse. In addition charge nurses cannot compel extra resources and are, therefore, dependent upon the nursing officer interpreting her/his needs. However, informal controls operate as well as formal ones. Goffman (1961) said of total institutions, that by their very rigidity they generate counter policies among inmates which, while the constraints remain unchallenged, enable inmates to find their own ways around these constraints. Although today's hospitals do not reflect Goffman's total institution concept absolutely, it is possible to examine some of the potential areas of dysfunction in the light of this theory. Thus it may be postulated that the charge nurse, who, for the patient, is the nurse operating as a "professional" nurse, has available two methods of control (doctor—charge nurse and nursing officer—charge nurse). These may be manipulated to act in opposition to each other, thus leaving the charge nurse slightly more room to manoeuvre in developing mechanisms to avoid constraints she/he may consider to be dysfunctional.

Austen (1978) writing of the present organisation of nursing services concluded that the rational system of management for nurses is designed to offer the rewards of career development and higher salary to nurses who are professionally orientated towards a value system different from nursing and this may well identify the nurse as reaching the apex of "professional" achievement at charge nurse level. If the intrinsic rewards of autonomy and expertise operate at this level, nurses may not regard hierarchical advancement as necessarily part of professional development. Thus, while nursing organisation benefits from a rational management system, the professional nurse regards the organisation as functioning to enable her/him to deliver nursing care to the patient with the minimum of disruption. The compulsion of senior nurses to feel responsible for all the actions undertaken by nurse practitioners of a less senior grade and to view such nurses as imbued with a lack of responsibility, discussed by Menzies (1960) and MacGuire (1964) complicates the situation at operational level, which is to say, in the wards or departments where the charge nurse is in control. Bendall (1973) considered that professionalism was affecting nurses. She noted that this striving for professional status was not motivating all groups of nurses at the same pace—thus she stated that teachers and managers of nurses were exhibiting these aspirations to a greater degree than clinical nurses. Fretwell (1980) writing of charge nurses and professional status considered that nursing is in a transitional state and is moving towards professional status as along a continuum. Chapter 3 examines some of the literature relating to professionalism so that further insight can be gained in considering this influence on nursing.

CHAPTER 3

Aspirations of Nursing

"To some extent the definition of a profession rests upon the degree to which its members can convince the public that it is one." (Pinker, 1978).

3.1 To Profess to Nurse

Felgate (1977) told us there is semantic confusion surrounding the word profession and even in its technical sense the definition of a professional occupation is fraught with misunderstanding. Carr-Saunders and Wilson (1933) noted that, historically, the acquisition of a liberal education, undertaken in the renowned universities equipped men to enter "the professions". At this time, when army commissions needed to be purchased and means were required to maintain the lifestyle appropriate to rank, army officers were considered, with members of the judiciary and ordained members of the established church, to have professional status. The present necessity for qualification, control and ethical standards came later and indeed, heralded the present struggle for "professional" status aspired to by many of today's occupations. As has been noted in Chapter 1 in medicine the vicissitudes affecting the variety of practitioners eventually resolved itself when social pressures demanded a more effective and, therefore, a more organised service. The Medical Act of 1858 provided the basis needed and the appropriate certification entitled the doctor to practise as a general practitioner. Further improvements in training developed from the efforts of the members of the profession themselves, when they recognised the need for expert specialist skills to be grounded in a broad based general education at university level. The lead given to medical practitioners by this development has enabled them to remain the leading professionals among health workers.

A tendency has developed, in recent years, to provide recipes for professional status, and to examine occupations in the light of such recipes, indicating that a little more of the ingredient service, or status or control of entrants or less hierarchical control or use of motor skills would make the mixture right. Thus Hall (1973) asserted of nursing that:

1. It provides a service to society involving specialised knowledge and skills.

40

2. It possesses a unique body of knowledge which it constantly seeks to extend, in order to improve its service.
3. It educates its own practitioners.
4. It sets its own standards.
5. It adapts its service to meet changing needs.
6. It accepts responsibility for safeguarding the public it serves.
7. It strives to made economical use of its practitioners.
8. It promotes the welfare and wellbeing of its practitioners and safeguards their interests.
9. It is motivated more by its commitment to the service it renders than by considerations of economic gain.
10. It adheres to a code of conduct based on ethical principles.
11. It unites for strength in achieving its larger purpose.
12. It is self governing.

and concluded that nursing does not yet contain all the ingredients for full professional status but is moving towards such a goal. Pepper (1977) however, discussing the inadequacy of such trait definitions, contended that not only nursing is deficient but also other high status occupations such as medicine are deficient by these measures. She posited other conditions which more efficiently define professional occupations and referring to medicine stated that:

1. The majority of practitioners have families of high social status.
2. A predominance of male practitioners.

and that this combination forms the criterion for professionalism. There is an impression here that the desire for enhanced status by nurses is in itself suspect and is perhaps being identified by Pepper as a rejection of "vocational" nursing, which Williams (1978) associated with Victorian society's acceptance of a service which required a total submission and eradication of self. Dingwell and McIntosh (1978) related this to the religiosity of Victorian England which legitimised the emergence of nursing as a respectable occupation for women. The structure of nursing then was the product of the social situation within which it emerged. It is useful, however, to recall that Merton (1960) (Chapter 2, 2.1) saw the seeking of professional status with its social accolade of autonomy as a legitimate human development. This development may be more in keeping with today's social mores and more acceptable to nurses who have experienced nursing only in its post Salmon Report structure.

Wilensky (1964) analysing professionalism, noted that "scientists" are judged by other scientists and "professionals" are judged by their clients. He also implied that professionalism is a developmental state which occupations can strive towards; citing autonomy, status, control of standards, control of training as factors which may operate in degree only, at certain stages of development, which indicates agreement with

41

Hall as quoted already. Wilensky also stated that professionals operating in a bureaucratic organisation are at risk to certain strains, since there is a tendency for autonomy to decrease and the service ideal to be eroded within a bureaucratic structure. Blau and Scott (1963) discussed professionalism in terms of opportunity for decision making based on objective criteria, specific expertise in a strictly limited area and affective neutrality. Present trends in nursing, however, view the lack of emotional involvement suggested by the attribute "affective neutrality" as antipathic to the adequate functioning of the nurse. Blau and Scott (1963) also recognised professional status as being achieved rather than ascribed and being associated with the client's benefit rather than the practitioner's, thus reinforcing Wilensky's findings. Carr-Sanders and Wilson (1933) also recognised a profession, not as a "sociological abstraction" but as an occupation with essential interest and importance to the public and it is because of the status attached to these groupings that occupations attempt to join such ranks and create pressure for professional acknowledgement. Such views differ somewhat from Etzioni's (1969) who saw some occupations as permanently deficient in the necessary attributes of professionalism by reason of their preponderance of women, hierarchical structure or by the lack of time devoted to training (which implies deficiency in the body of knowledge available). He included nursing among these occupations. There is, however, a degree of absolutism in such categorisation which creates difficulties in acceptance since all the factors mentioned are subject to change and in nursing have certainly changed over the years. The men/women ratio is changing. The hierarchical structure in nursing is very much an administrative convenience and has been changed before. The effect of the hierarchy on bedside nursing, which is where professional nursing is undertaken, is probably no more than the constraints operating upon any group of workers who work with constraints set by the district management teams (Rowbottom, 1971). However, Pepper (1977) who studied learner nurses in some depth in two wards in one hospital, concluded that they lacked autonomy over their practice. Interestingly from this she deduced that trained nurses also lack autonomy, but the conclusion is difficult to support from the evidence offered.

Specialist knowledge seems to be a quality to which all professionals must have access. Katz (1969) writing of knowledge, its hoarding and its use, said of nursing in the United States that:

> "Hospitals are in short, under pressure to implement existing knowledge but at the same time involved in controlling knowledge. Physicians are chiefly responsible for deciding which items of knowledge are safe to use— safe for the patients and safe for their own reputations and the reputation of the hospital."

Katz went on to state that hospital administrators are responsible for deciding which bits of knowledge are too expensive to use and, therefore, saw both the physician and the administrator in hospital as possessing knowledge and power (at least power over the application of knowledge) and that nurses accept the legitimacy of the doctors' control over knowledge. Ferguson (1976) made something of the same point when she noted

". . . society has always invested the nature of learning with high status for those who are seen to have knowledge invariably also hold the power."

Katz (1969) in relation to nurses, further noted that some nurses are aware of the element of control existing in the deprivation of knowledge and suggested that doctors are wary of nurses who are interested in acquiring more knowledge, since, he contended, doctors see nurses in the role of buffer or sponge which protects doctors from the consequences of inappropriate action or inaction. It is not possible to state if such a degree of passivity also exists among nurses in this country, although Dodd (1973) described charge nurses acting in this way. However, Katz (1969) and Kelly (1966) also noted that nurses consciously recognise an area of patient care which is exclusively in their control. Nurses assess the patients' nursing needs, identify priorities in the delivery of care to meet these needs and organise the delivery of this care. Priorities in medically prescribed treatments are also identified and treatment carried out accordingly. Other services to the patient are also co-ordinated by the nurse in charge of wards and departments. Nurses make decisions in these matters which are referred neither to doctors nor to the nursing hierarchy. In this country schools of nursing may and do specify particular procedures which learner nurses must follow and this may create anxieties for charge nurses whose expertise may advocate other approaches. These are unresolved dilemmas but such conflict relates to the teaching of others not to the practice undertaken by the charge nurse and other permanent staff.

The belief expressed by Pinker (1978) with which this Chapter is introduced tells us that the public confers professional status but not why the public confers such status. For nursing the demands made upon charge nurses at ward level are considerable. These demands require not only an adequate knowledge base but an awareness that medical, biological and social sciences are in a dynamic developing state and all of these affect the nurse (Chapman, 1974). Henderson (1980) said of these developments that technical skills increase in number and complexity and include physical and psychosocial evaluations and diagnostic tests, assisting with pre and post surgical care that involves the operation of sensitive and dangerous machines; also the administration of drugs whose numbers proliferate hourly and whose possible threats to human welfare should haunt those who give and those who take them. This state of change and conflict, expansion of knowledge, extension of role within which a charge nurse must operate demands that consideration be given to the need for the practitioner to have adequate opportunity for systematic updating if competence in nursing is to be maintained. Section 3.2 pursues this point by examining the literature dealing specifically with this particular need of trained nurses.

3.2 Why Education?

Drucker (1965) said of educational development that it becomes a priority of national policy because education controls a country's military, technological and economic potential. Even more is there a likelihood of the good health of the populace influencing a country's military, technological and economic potential, for example, the poor health status of recruits for military service during the Boer War gave cause for concern when it became necessary to build a larger army, (Gilbert, 1966). The conjunction of health and education occurs when the training of staff for the health services is considered. The Report of the Royal Commission on Medical Education (1968) tells us that:

"... all doctors in whatever branch of medicine, must have the opportunity and the time for continuing education in order to keep up to date in their own field and to remain reasonably well acquainted with development in others."

An earlier report, the Sub-Committee of the Standing Nursing Advisory Committee (1966) suggested that the concept of systematic and progressive education for the registered nurse had received little recognition, and considered that any educational facilities made available should recognise that home commitments and part time work imposes constraints upon staff which influences their ability to take advantage of updating courses; a factor which can be identified in the findings of the present research. More recently, the International Council of Nurses stated in 1976:

"The nurse carries personal responsibility for nursing practice and for maintaining competence by continual learning."

It is to identify what opportunity is available to nurses to undertake this responsibility that the present research has been undertaken.

Cooper (1970) argues that nurses as well as doctors continue professional education in many ways, citing: 1. shared experience; 2. use of journals; 3. seminars; 4. university programmes.

She noted that medical advances have forced doctors to continue learning if they wish to keep up to date and that such current medical advances demand different types of nursing skills, so that the nurse also must be a continuing learner. Darmastaater (1977) said that skills needed by professions change rapidly and that there is every indication that they will continue to do so. She considered another aspect of post-

44

basic education for nurses; the quality of the programmes offered. In questioning the quality of such training in the United States she reminded us that the patient is potentially the real sufferer since the patient is at the mercy of a practitioner's skills and abilities. Lysault (1970) and Burgess (1978) also advised nurses in the United States to be sceptical regarding the quality of education programmes available.

In this country the Joint Board of Clinical Nursing Studies was set up in 1970 to offer a national system of post-basic clinical education for nurses. The terms of reference were:

> "To consider and advise on the clinical needs of nurses and midwives for post-basic clinical training in specialist aspects of the hospital and community nursing services in England and Wales; to co-ordinate and supervise the courses provided as a result of such advice; and to discharge such other functions as we may assign to them. The Joint Board has the power to co-opt additional members for specific purposes and to appoint sub-committees as necessary."

The Board offers a wide range of specialist courses of varying timespan and some of the courses offer certificates of competence in the specialty, others offer certificates of attendance only. The education programmes available are very flexible. Some extend over periods of 6–12 months; other courses are a mixture of day release combined with an introductory period of study; again, others occupy only a few days. Courses are offered with Joint Board approval in many centres, for example, schools of nursing and colleges of technology throughout England and Wales. In 1975 more than 800 certificates of competence were awarded to nurses from these specialty courses. The terms of reference of the Board confine its activity to education in nursing specialist areas and the Board has not been able to offer any updating in these specialties, since resources are concentrated on meeting an initial need. The Board is not designed to provide general updating for nursing staff in the non-specialist fields of nursing. However, the third report of the Board states:

> ". . . this would include opportunities for further education and training in the practice of nursing for all qualified."

Green (1978) confirmed that there is little formal education open to nurses beyond registration and cited one regional health authority's expenditure as follows:

TABLE 2
Post-basic Educational Expenditure

Category	Numbers	Expenditure
Medical	2,391	£25,000
Nursing	28,665	£50,000

Smart (1974) writing of doctors, noted the rapid increase in attendance when seniority payments were tied to continuing education. This relates in some ways to Berg's (1973) finding that continuing education for nurses also needs "reward". She considered that there is a need to associate continuing learning with promotion possibilities and/or acknowledgement by seniors. Berg also identified desire for professional knowledge as a motivating factor and Goldiak (1977) writing of continuing education for nurses in Israel, was adamant that this is essential for professional competence. In Israel, she reported that attendance at up-dating courses is acknowledged by credits which are recognised for salary benefits. In the United States there is a movement towards a systematic, continuing education process related to relicensing, (Roem, 1974).

In an increasing number of States the introduction of continuing education units represents hours of post-basic education. Usually, 10 contact hours equal one continuing education unit and varying numbers of units, acquired over periods of two to three years, are demanded by these States before relicensing can take place.

There is no indication that, in this country, interest is being taken in a systematic record of individual nurses updating nursing knowledge on a cumulative basis. Indeed, Auld (1979) speaking to nurses attending the Royal College of Nursing Research Society's annual conference said of nursing that

". . . it continues to educate itself largely by a process of osmosis."

In effect, also, the recommendations of the Salmon Report (1966) moved the emphasis from clinical updating to management education for charge nurses.

It is perhaps worth considering at this point what Bilodeau (1969) said of retraining needs in industry. He stated that it is possible to estimate the cost of retraining (and this can also be said to apply to updating) but it is not possible to evaluate the price paid for not retraining. Merton (1957) also touched on this when he referred to trained incapacity as a state of affairs when abilities function as inadequacies or blindspots. This occurs when actions based on training and skills which have been successfully applied in the past may result in inappropriate behaviour in changed conditions. Chapman (1976) indicated that the increasing body of knowledge from the behavioural sciences has made it possible for health service staff, such as charge nurses, to develop more understanding of patients as people. This knowledge also permeates society and may result in patients developing new expectations of charge nurses. Unmet expectations may generate anxieties, which have been noted by others, (Chapter 2, 2.1) and these affect nursing behaviours. Such behaviours may in turn affect the speed of patients' recovery and, therefore, have implications

46

for the consumption of resources, both human and financial, which takes us back to Bilodeau's observations noted earlier in this section.

Chapter 1, 1.2 gives the topics set for examination by the General Nursing Council in 1923. Roper (1976) investigating the training of nurses for the Register, stated that there has been little change in the three year syllabus of training although there has been change in the terminology used, with change from the designation of learner nurses as probationers to students and the fact that the term education has superseded training as a description of the process by which nurses learn their skills. Roper also noted that the percentage of time spent in formal learning increased from 10% to 17% but that the total hours available were reduced due to the shorter working week. She also recognised that even if the syllabus has not drastically changed it has expanded and the increase in material to be covered is being squeezed into a restricted time package. She also discussed the impact of secondment to specialist areas for training, as in psychiatic and obstetric areas and posited that this places additional strains upon learners whose training is still an apprentice type training, when most of them will practice in the general field. In France, Collière (1980) wondered if nursing is based on a body of knowledge which provides information about the life of people, their habits, their beliefs and their relationships or if it relies on a single unique source of explanation for illness. In Ireland, Staunton (1979) suggested that emphasis in nursing has moved from pre-occupation with bodily ministrations to responding to the patient's, physical and psychological reactions. In this country, Chapman, McFarlane, Pembrey and Ogier, among others, have, as has already been noted, emphasised this need for interpersonal skills in nurses but the commitments of the training programmes make adequate training in these skills difficult to accomplish during the three years available for basic training.

The preceding review of the literature suggests that not only is basic training in nursing inadequate to equip nurses to operate at the level of charge nurse but also suggests that the changes which are taking place in society and in medical science have implications for nursing which are of particular importance for the nurses who are responsible for the organisation of patient care. In addition to these recognisable needs it is worth speculating on what benefits might accrue from the encouragement of pleasurable, intellectual curiosity among practitioners, since Whitehead (1932) writing of science suggested that advancement here is almost wholly the outgrowth of such curiosity.

3.3 Summary of Literature Search

The preceding Chapters have used the literature to draw a framework within which the service of nursing can be identified. Sources taken from the history of nursing and from role theory have attempted to define the nurse in the social setting of the hospital and to clarify the confusion that surrounds the organisational structure of nursing. Literature relating to professionalism generally has been used to help understanding of the incipient professionalism which can be recognised within the occupation as it now exists. Literature relating to nursing and to the grades of nurse examined in the present study have been consulted to establish the present state of nursing and to indicate that the pressures of stress and change which affect society generally are also reflected in the state of nursing. The key position of the charge nurse in the control of the delivery of care to the patient has been recognised.

No attempt has been made to provide a history of nursing and current controversies regarding the rightness or otherwise of the claims of those seeking professional status, in a sociological sense, has been but lightly touched upon. The researcher has assumed that social groupings, such as nurses, reflect society generally and may seek social rewards for services by the means offered by society and that the seeking of professional status may be part of the developmental process of nursing.

The literature cited indicates the clarity and the ambiguities which exist in nursing and identify the complexities which are to be found in the hospital setting. The development of new roles and the realignment of older roles has been noted and the need for a recognised method of enabling nursing knowledge to be increased and updated had been identified. This monograph sets out to investigate the views of nurses of two grades and two specialties in relation to the updating of nursing knowledge and uses a survey approach.

CHAPTER 4

Methodology

4.1 Access to Districts

The object of this research was to identify the views of trained nurses regarding their ability to keep up to date with nursing knowledge. It is, therefore, consumer orientated research and the design of the project and the identification of relevant variables emerged from the literature and from the experience of the researcher.

A social survey approach was considered appropriate since the data required were needed to describe a social reality. Moser and Kalton (1972) identified social surveys as concerned with the demographic characteristics, the social environment, the activities or opinions and attitudes of some groups of people. The present research was concerned with a particular group—trained nurses. The trained nurse category was reduced further and subgroups identified. These were:

Specialty— only those in general nursing divisions and midwifery divisions were involved.

Grade — only two grades were examined,
a. Charge Nurse the nurse in charge of a ward or its equivalent.
b. Nursing Officer—the nurse in charge of a group of wards forming one Unit.

The population from which the sample was drawn was the staff of these grades employed in one regional health authority. The sample size of 400 represented 10% of the nurses of relevant grades in post. The numbers of staff available were obtained from statistics collated in the region and the 400 sample was stratified to include the correct proportion of nurses from the districts included in the sample.

The original intention of the researcher to use three health districts to represent all health districts was modified in the light of experience. The sample was required to include hospitals, large, small, rural and urban, whose nurses were in the control of nurse managers of general and midwifery divisions. The inability of the teaching district (that health district containing the Medical Training School) to participate in the research necessitated a different approach since the absence of the wide range of hospitals existing in the teaching district made the proposed sample unrepresentative of the health region generally. Details of the sampling procedure decided are given later in section 4.2.

All district nursing officers of the districts selected (six in number) subsequently agreed to participate in the research and all of these nurses made the research known to subordinate staff which enabled the researcher to make specific arrangements with the hospitals involved.

There were three main methods available to the researcher to inform the staff who made up the sample of the aims of the research and what it required of respondents. The nurse managers in the different health districts decided which method they endorsed and the researcher took advantage of whatever opportunities were available.

The three approaches were:

1. A meeting was arranged by the district nursing officer which enabled the researcher to approach key people and to make arrangements to visit the hospitals where other meetings were arranged at which questionnaires could be distributed.

2. A nursing officer introduced the researcher to the staff who were part of the sample and thus facilitated the delivery of the questionnaires.

3. The researcher was invited to visit the hospitals and deliver the questionnaires. Various techniques were used to identify the people in the sample and this varied from asking the nurse in charge of each unit visited, where the staff in the sample were located, to asking a helpful charge nurse to locate the appropriate wards. Secretaries in nursing offices were also helpful in this way.

Although the methods of access differed between health districts and also between hospitals, in all cases the researcher's visits had been legitimised and appointments to meet staff both for the delivery of questionnaires and for interviews were made, if not without difficulty, at least without any hitches. The sampling frame in all cases was the "Nominal Roll" a computer printout available to finance departments to identify nurses so that salaries could be paid.

Sussman (1971) noted that there is client revolt against all research (in the United States of America) stating that all target populations want some sort of pay-off for being researched. In the present study the author noted some indications of this from the nurses involved since it was clearly demonstrated that these nurses wanted some acknowledgement of their cooperation in the form of a report to the health district of the findings of the study and it was agreed to make this available.

As has been stated, one regional health authority was interested in the research and a regional nursing officer introduced the subject at a meeting with district nursing officers so that the health districts included in the sample were thus notified that the research project was being considered.

The Population

This comprised nurses of nursing officer and charge nurse grade in the midwifery and general divisions in one regional health authority.

4.2 The Sample

Mann (1971) says of sampling that it is necessary because, in real life, it is often not possible to collect information about every case and that sampling saves time and labour but replaces certainty with probability. The object of sampling is to produce, from a smaller number, information which represents the views of the population from which the sample was taken.

In the present research a "cluster sampling" approach was made. Brown (1958) said of cluster sampling that it contains units which are aggregates of natural units. She suggested that a school is an example of such an aggregate and in the present research health districts from different geographic environments throughout the health region were used in the way that Brown recommended schools be used.

The health districts contained hospitals of various sizes and these were located from the metropolis to the coast and were from eastern and western boundaries. The hospitals were in both urban and rural areas.

The method used to select the sample was systematic sampling. Here each name of the appropriate grade and specialty on the nominal roll was given a number from tables of random numbers (Dixon and Massey, 1969) and appropriate sized samples were selected from each health district.

The selection of the sub-sample for interviewing took place on the first day the researcher arrived in each health district. The names of all appropriate staff available during the time the researcher was in the district were put in a box and random selection by the lottery method was used to select the proportion allocated from each district. Nursing officers and charge nurses were selected separately. Randomisation was relied upon to maintain the representativeness of other variables.

It is necessary to note that as a sampling frame the nominal roll had limitations, since staff who have left the organisation remain on the roll for varying periods of time in case salary adjustments are required following pay awards. This was unknown to the researcher at the time and resulted in 21 questionnaires being returned as "not employed in this district". This reduced the sample to 379.

Stratification of the Sample

In order to take account of the variations in the size of districts, numbers of staff in the different grades, the distribution of staff between large hospitals and small hospitals and the numbers employed in the two specialties involved, the sample was stratified in each district to select the appropriate proportions from each group. Size of hospital was considered by deciding arbitrarily that large hospitals contained 200 or more beds and small hospitals fewer than 200 beds. Mann (1971) said of stratification that it safeguards the representativeness of the sample by ensuring that the known groups in the population are represented fairly in the sample.

4.3 Data Collection

Two methods were used:

1. *Questionnaire.*

These were delivered in envelopes which contained stamped envelopes addressed to the researcher. There was also an introductory letter to reinforce the information given when the questionnaires were delivered. (Appendix C). Whenever possible the questionnaires were delivered personally by the researcher. Oppenheim (1966) said of this method of delivery that it ensures a high response rate by giving the benefit of personal contact. When, because of absence due to holidays or sickness, this personal distribution was not possible, arrangements were made with unit nursing officers to have the questionnaires delivered. In some cases secretaries offered to ensure delivery.

The response rate to the 284 questionnaires which were returned represented a 75% rate of response.

Grebnik (1970) said that mailing questionnaires enables large numbers of respondents to be reached quickly but drew attention to the acute problem of non response and Oppenheim (1966) reminded us that non response is not a random process. In the present research non response was first tackled by personal delivery (as has already been stated) but the limitations on time operating prevented any attempt to reduce non response further except by posting reminder cards. These cards increased the response from 71% to 75%.

2. *Interview.*

The main tool of the present research was the questionnaire developed for the research but, in order to increase understanding of the data collected, another approach, that of interviewing, was undertaken. Ten percent of the sample randomly selected were interviewed. The interviews were constructed around a checklist based on the questionnaire with some additional related subjects. The checklist was used as a guideline and respondents were asked to review the questionnaire before the interview took place. A spare questionnaire was available during interviews for those who did not bring the questionnaire with them. If the topics from the checklist were not mentioned spontaneously by the interviewees they were introduced by the researcher.

During the pilot stage it was verified that it took 45 minutes to cover adequately all that needed to be discussed. In practice most interviews took longer, many lasting more than two hours. Appointments were made with the staff involved and interviews were arranged to suit the interviewee. The venue proved difficult in some cases, but since all that was needed was reasonable privacy and a period without interruption, the use of ward offices, coffee rooms and gardens proved suitable. Staff changing rooms were used on two occasions. When ward duty rooms were used during the pilot stage it was found that the interview was subjected to frequent interruption. Notes were taken during interviews, with the respondents permission. All those selected for interview agreed to participate.

Other Interviews

In approaching hospitals throughout the region to make appointments to visit staff to distribute questionnaires a number of interviews, in addition to those required to introduce the research to the district, took place. The senior nurses in many hospitals sought interviews. Some of these were mainly of a social nature, others were directed to obtaining more information about the research or the researcher. These interviews were not recorded but gave the researcher considerable insight into the degree of anxiety felt by those nurses who were in charge of (mainly small) hospitals whose functions were changing or whose administrative allegiance had changed in the recent past. The anxieties these nurses expressed were remarkably consistent throughout the region and no doubt reflected the threat of change and loss of status that then confronted health service staff in all health regions. This threat is at present increasing rather than being reduced.

4.4 Scales Used

From the literature no appropriate scale of measurement of nurses' satisfaction with updating facilities available to enable them to maintain competence was identified and a simple self-rating scale called a "satisfaction thermometer" was devised for the research. The scale was 100 mm long marked at the lower end "very dissatisfied" and at the upper end "very satisfied". There were two scales used:

Scale 1 measured satisfaction with journal/library availability.
Scale 2 measured satisfaction with post basic educational updating facilities available. These scales are illustrated below.

Respondents were asked to mark at the level they felt appropriate between the two points. The researcher later applied a score to these

FIGURE 4

Satisfaction/Dissatisfaction Scale

very satisfied

very dissatisfied

scales. The measure ranged from 0 to 100. Scores of 25 or below were categorised as dissatisfied and those of above 75 were categorised as satisfied. It is appreciated that the ordinal nature of such scales is a limitation on their power to discriminate between closely related scores and it is for this reason that scores from the extremes of the scales only were used to describe respondents views. Moser and Kalton (1972) said of such scales that they are more sensitive than straight "Yes" "No" responses. They also stressed the danger of "central tendency response" in such scales but considered that they are useful because they are easy to operate. The decision to use only the extremes of the scales is based on Moser and Kalton's comments modified by the results obtained during pretesting of the questionnaires. There was no evidence that the error of central tendency did, in fact, operate when the scales were used.

Reliability

Moser and Kalton (1972) said of reliability that it is the measure of the ability of a scale to give the same results when used under constant conditions. In this research the test and retest method of examining the reliability of the scales was used. Abdellah and Levine (1965) considered that the test and retest method can adequately be used to measure the effectiveness of the measurement tool used in social research.

In the present research a group of State Registered Nurses attending a course at a technical college outside the catchment area agreed to participate in the tesing of the questionnaire. The group were asked only to cooperate in the research and the ten nurses who agreed were given the questionnaire to complete. The objectives of the research were explained and permission was requested to return to undertake some further work at a later date. When the completed questionnaires were collected arrangements were made to return in ten days time to continue the work.

The same questionnaires were distributed during the second visit. The colour of the paper was changed but otherwise no differences existed.

The correlation coefficient was 0·92 on Scale 1 and 0·90 on Scale 2. These represent what Brown (1958) described as coefficients of stability. Krausz and Miller (1974) reminded us that the second application of the test may have been influenced by the original use of the scale. It is accepted that in the present research it is unlikely that such contamination was completely reduced but in discussion with the group after the completion of the second questionnaire it was apparent that at a conscious level the nurses were unaware that the two questionnaires were identical.

Validity

Of validity, Abdellah and Levine (1965) stated that data are valid if they actually measure what they are supposed to measure and advised that in some cases of research into nursing it may be necessary to use a panel of experts as a means of examining the validity of the intruments. In the present research this approach was used, therefore, face validity only was tested. The limitations on this approach were accepted.

Two experienced nurse researchers were consulted during the development of the questionnaire and their views ascertained as to the ability of the questions to generate the required data. The completed questionnaire was presented to a second panel of nurses during the first visit to the technical college. The questionnaire was distributed to be read by ten nurses and the objectives of the research were stated. The panel met the researcher after an hour and the usefulness of the questions in eliciting the type of data required was discussed. There was at least 75% agreement on all questions and this was accepted by the researcher in the absence of other criteria for validation as a satisfactory basis on which to proceed.

The Questionnaire

There were 23 questions asked of respondents and these were a mixture of dichotomous questions with space left for elaboration of replies and open ended questions. Question 19 used two four point scales to elicit information. The "satisfaction thermometers" have already been discussed. The unstructured questions produced data which were categorised by the researcher (for details see Chapter 5).

Stacey (1969) suggested that the use of a variety of methods to elicit data from respondents enriches the findings of research and a further attempt at this enrichment was made by asking for the respondents' views on the need for the updating of nursing knowledge. Content analysis was used to order the additional data collected from these replies.

It is appreciated that the data collected in the present research are only applicable to the regional health authority in which the data were collected but it is considered that the findings may be of interest to nurses from other regional health authorities.

CHAPTER 5

Information on Educational Programmes

5.1 Who Needs Updating?

Davies (1980) considered that there are signs that nurses are becoming aware of information needs at clinical, educational and management level and this was of interest in the present research. Twenty per cent of the respondents felt themselves to be in great need of updating. Statistically significant differences existed between: those qualified for less than five years (37%) and those qualified 25 or more years (14%). Ninety-four per cent overall, felt in need of some updating whilst only 14% recorded that adequate opportunity was available to them.

Bendall (1975) discussing the educational needs of trained nurses at a conference at Nottingham University, regretted the divisions which had developed between nurses who concentrated upon education and those who were involved in patient care, since one result of this could be, she considered, a lack of awareness by practising nurses of a need for continuing education, as they lacked close contact with educationists within the profession. The responses recorded in this research, while not dispelling these fears entirely, suggested that many nurses are aware of a need to update and seem to be in agreement with O'Connor (1979) who cited The National Commission for the Study of Nursing and Nurse Education (1970) when she stated;

" . . . technological advances altered aspects of practice and care delivery and social changes in the health professions and the larger culture would combine to make lifelong learning a practical necessity."

O'Connor was writing of the United States of America but such a statement has relevance for this country also since social change and technological advance apply in both societies.

5.2 What Needs Updating?

Respondents most frequently identified a need for:

1. General clinical updating: Overall 25% of respondents recorded this. Statistically significant differences existed between the responses

of: midwives (12%) and others (27%). This difference may indicate the effectiveness of the obligation upon midwives to attend updating courses every five years. No other statistically significant differences were observed.

2. Interpersonal skills: Twenty-two per cent of respondents recorded a need for training in interpersonal skills.

Quenzer (1974) noted in her study that nurses were unaware that interpersonal skills could be used therapeutically for patients and Dodd (1973) found that nursing staff, in the main, did not consider that such skills could be inculcated during educational programmes. In Israel, Bergman (1979) when examining the educational needs of unit head nurses (a group she equates with charge nurses in this country), found that such nurses identified human relations skills as first in order of importance in training needs.

In the present research the question asked was:

"Could you list any subjects which you consider could usefully be studied by nurses in charge of wards or departments to help them develop and maintain the skills required of them."

The replies categorised as "interpersonal skills" were identified by the researcher from the following seven groups of responses:

a. Need to understand patients' anxieties.
b. Need to help staff understand patients' needs. (This included reference to social and psychological aspects).
c. Need to know how to support relatives in periods of great stress e.g. bereavement.
d. Need to know how to relate to relatives generally.
e. Need to know how to integrate staff into the ward team.
f. Need to know how to make the ward team cohere.
g. Need to know how to help other groups understand ward needs.

As in Bergman's (1979) study it can be seen that in this research nurses did give high priority to these factors without labelling them precisely. It may be that changes in society generally are the precipitating elements here since nurse training, historically, while acknowledging the importance of an empathetic approach to patient care has been able to devote little time, in a crowded curriculum, to developing these skills.

Statistically significant differences were observed between the following groups in respect of the need for interpersonal skills: those with dependents (16%) those with no dependents (27%); while males recorded 14% and females 27%.

The interval since qualification produced differences: of those qualified less than 15 years 30% identified a need; of those qualified 15 or more years 15% identified a need.

It is possible that people with dependents and also those who have a number of years' experience may feel that they have acquired such skills by means of their life's experience. There is, perhaps a danger here in assuming that all lives yield sufficient experience to enable people to develop such skills and that others will be capable of internalising the experience to enable them to develop these necessary skills.

3. Teaching skills: Twelve per cent of respondents recorded a need for teaching skills. Eight respondents had training as nurse teachers, either having clinical teachers certificates or were Registered Nurse Tutors. Another 30 respondents (13% of the sample) had attended three to five day programmes described either as art of teaching, examining or teaching and examining.

Marson (1979) writing of nurse training in the United Kingdom said that it is assumed that nurses learn as they work and from this she made a further assumption, that trained nurses teach. Fretwell (1980) tested this in her study of the ward as a learning environment and concluded that the charge nurse both creates and controls this aspect of ward experience for nurses in training. Goddard (1963) noted that charge nurses spent little measurable time in interaction with learners. Lelean (1973) also commented on the small proportion of the ward sister's time which was spent in informal communications with learner nurses. Two per cent was the proportion observed. A further 14–22 minutes per day on average were spent on formal communications (giving of reports etc) in each ward. Lelean also noted that 20 communications an hour were liable to fragment the charge nurses' time and suggested that this pattern leaves little time for teaching. Revans (1962) also noted the multivariate demands on the ward sister and the paucity of time actually available to be spent with learner nurses. These studies suggest that where there is little interaction there can be little teaching and Lamond (1974) said of learner nurses that they recorded the charge nurse as potential teacher in only one third of possible choices. Also, Catnach and Houghton (1961) in their study of methods of teaching in nurse training schools did not observe any incident which they categorised as "teaching" by charge nurses during the month in which their data were collected. However, Schurr (1968) reflected the charge nurses' views on this with the quoted comment, "Whatever we do we are always teaching." Pembrey (1978) seemed to support this. Fretwell (1980) also, in her exhaustive study of the ward as a learning environment, recorded that the time spent by charge nurses in the teaching of learners was observed to vary from 1% to 13% of the time available.

Respondents in the present research gave relatively low priority to the acquisition of teaching skills and in response to the question, "Are there any programmes available to you to enable you to develop the teaching skills required of you in your ward or department?" some mentioned role models; doctors, sisters, other nurses. Others stated that to train as a nurse enabled the nurse to develop teaching skills for use in the ward situation. Overall 12% of respondents recorded a need for training in teaching skills. There were statistically significant differences between: those qualified for less than five years, 20% of whom recorded this need, and those qualified for 25 or more years, 6% of whom recorded this need.

There are indications from this and from other studies, (Goddard, 1963; Lelean, 1973; Lamond, 1974; Fretwell, 1980) that no clear understanding exists of the role of the charge nurse in the teaching of learners. Indeed Marson (1979) stated that a frequently heard comment from charge nurses interviewed in her study was " . . . if I had wanted to teach I would have taken a nurse tutor course." Marson posited that if the emphasis was moved from "teaching" as a didactic activity and placed on "learning" as a personal development, some of these difficulties would be overcome; a plea for a facilitator of learning rather than a teacher. Ogier (1979) drew somewhat similar conclusions from her research stating that emphasis should be placed on training in interpersonal skills to enable charge nurses to meet the learning needs of nurses in training. The lack of consensus between the expectations of the educationists and the perceptions of charge nurses is in need of further exploration. During a period when research indicates the increasing multiplicity of demands upon the available time of the charge nurse, increasing emphasis has also been placed upon the teaching aspects of the role. Lelean (1973) suggested that the implications in terms of time of the teaching component of the charge nurse role should be acknowledged and catered for or the lack of available time should be duly accepted and adequate alternative arrangements made.

Other skills needed which were less frequently recorded.

1. Specialist skills—10% recorded.
   This category described needs associated with specialist areas of work and included reference to updating in theatre work, intensive therapy, neurological, renal and coronary care knowledge.
2. Technical skills—5% recorded.
   This category described knowledge needed to manage equipment and included reference to monitoring equipment used in assessment, diagnosis and therapy.
3. Academic skills—4% recorded.
   This category included reference to the Diploma in Nursing, studies in sociology, psychology and biochemistry.

It was a surprising finding in this research that few respondents mentioned the Diploma in Nursing as a part of continuing education in nursing. Four respondents referred to the Diploma in Nursing. One had been awarded the Diploma and one the Advanced Diploma in

Midwifery. Two others mentioned this as a possible avenue for further study. This point is discussed further in the final Chapter of this book.

5.3 What Education is Available?

Three main sources were identified:
1. Clinical programmes (not held in district)
2. Local study episodes (one working day or a half working day)
3. Management Training.

Clinical Programmes

These programmes could be divided into three categories:
Category 1 which included nationally registered clinical training mainly for sub-divisions of the nurses' registered, but not exclusively this.
Category 2 which was almost entirely Joint Board of Clinical Nursing Studies Courses.
Category 3 which included conferences, specialist lectures other than those in home district produced by employing authority.

Local Study Episodes

These were programmes produced by the employing authority, were *ad hoc* in nature and occasionally consisted of a full day's study covering several topics or half a working day devoted to one topic. No respondents recorded any modular programmes or any related topics.

Management Training

All respondents who mentioned these courses had attended programmes provided by the regional health authority and no respondent referred to university, polytechnic or Royal College of Nursing courses.

The Salmon Report (1966) resulted in a change in the provision of management training programmes and all regional health authorities either by arrangement with other educational bodies or by means of their own staff colleges, provided some training in management skills.

The Salmon Report recommended management training for nurses in three stages:
1. First line management, consisting of two periods of two weeks designed to meet the needs of charge nurses.
2. Second line management, to meet the needs of nursing officers consisting of 12 weeks' tuition, again in two parts.
3. Top management courses, to meet the needs of more senior nurses, consisting of a further 12 weeks' study.

In the South West Thames Region, for example, management courses of two weeks' duration introduce staff to management concepts. Further modules of training of three to five days' duration concentrate on: the training aspects of the manager's role; effective presentation of information; staff development; interviewing; committee work.

The two week management course is designed to allow the students to study: programming and planning of work; personnel and employee relations; interpersonal skills and self-awareness; verbal communications, one to one and to group; written communication, reports and letters; objectives setting, performance appraisal; current issues in the National Health Service allocation and control of managerial resources.

Post-basic and Inservice Tutors

Question 12 in the questionnaire used in the survey asked:

"Is there a nurse specifically in charge of education for qualified nurses in your district?"

During the period of the survey there were three districts in the sample who had a nurse designated as a senior tutor, post-basic training or senior tutor, in-service training. Only 44% (124) answered this question. Ninety respondents said that there was such a tutor. Thirty came from districts which did not have such a post. Thirty said that there was not a tutor for post-basic education. Ten came from districts that had a tutor in post.

These data suggested that respondents either did not interpret the question correctly or that the presence of a tutor specifically responsible for this aspect of nurse education had, at the time of the survey, made little impact upon the districts generally. An increase in the number of such appointments within the region may well have given greater publicity within the districts to the existence of the post and brought about greater awareness. The lack of consistency in the responses means that the information must be treated with caution and these responses have not been included in the data entered for computer analysis.

5.4 Who Attended What Courses?

It was of interest to identify what proportions of the sample had recorded attendance at any post basic educational programme. Seventy-five per cent of respondents had attended management programmes. Fifty-eight per cent of respondents had attended clinical programmes.

Information on clinical programmes

Among the 42% of respondents who had not attended any post basic programmes in the clinical field there were statistically significant differences between the following groups: among married staff 51% had not attended formal post basic clinical programmes; while among unmarried staff the percentage was 26%. Of those working in the specialty geriatrics 68% had not attended a formal programme; while among those working in other areas 36% had not attended a formal programme.

Staff from maternity divisions did not only record 100% attendance at Category 1 courses, without which they would not be regarded as trained midwives, but they also recorded high levels of attendance at Category 2 and Category 3 courses. This is in addition to the mandatory requirement to attend a five day approved refresher course every five years.

Other interesting differences were indicated in respect of the type of nursing concerned: respondents working in geriatric areas recorded a lower proportion of respondents attending formal courses (Categories 1 and 2) but a higher proportion attending informal (Category 3) courses. Residents working in smaller hospitals also recorded this.

Some explanation for this may lie in the fact that informal programmes can often be arranged by the participants themselves and do not need the co-operation of the employing authority since they can be arranged during off-duty periods and this factor may also influence the response of married staff. Comments from respondents suggested that this certainly occurred.

Who has Attended Management Courses?

The data indicated that 75% of respondents had attended such courses. Statistically significant differences existed regarding attendance between: those on night duty (61%); those on day duty (75%); those working full time (79%); those working part time (62%).

Management Training and Participants' Expectations

Of the 213 respondents who attended management courses 52% recorded that these courses met their needs.

There were statistically significant differences between: nursing officers (general) (91%) and others (47%) whose needs were met. Nursing officers (maternity) also exhibited lower levels of satisfaction with these courses but the numbers were small and the differences did not reach significance.

The Courses Related to Work?

Fifty-one per cent of respondents considered that the courses attended related to work. There were statistically significant differences between the responses of: nursing officers (general) (91%) and others (45%).

Again nursing officers (maternity) recorded differently. No nursing officer in the maternity area considered that the course related to work. The numbers were small and not statistically significant but in view of the high participation of midwives in post-basic education this response may reflect high expectations which are not being met or it may indicate a lack of involvement by midwives in courses which do not enhance their knowledge of their own specialist field.

Further information was elicited from respondents regarding the course contents to establish what expectations if any were not being met and these were limited to information on:

1. Theory Content of the Course (defining theory as the exposition of the principles of a subject).

Sixty per cent considered that they required more theoretical content. It is possible that in the two weeks or so available to tutors it is not seen by them as practicable to place the management concepts being presented within a comprehensive framework of management theory but without an understanding of the various schools of thought which have contributed to this body of knowledge from scientific management through human relationships to the behavioural sciences, the information received may lack a reliable base and the enquiring nurse may well reject information which is not supported.

2. Practical Application of the Courses.

Fifty-seven per cent of respondents considered that the presentation of information on such courses needed more practical application. There were no significant differences between groups.

Pembrey (1978), writing of charge nurses' acquisition of management skills, reported that the development of these skills was not enhanced by attendance at management courses but such skills were developed among those who exhibited them through experience at staff nurse level and that these charge nurses had all identified a 'role model' from whom they had learned their management skills.

The present study does not fully support this finding. Indeed many respondents commented, both at interview and in the questionnaires, that (in addition to being an interesting experience) their attendance at management training courses had been valuable in stimulating them to develop new thinking and the most frequent comment was that the approach to teaching, which respondents identified as being informal, was suited to adults in a learning environment and was stated to be "encouraging". What seemed to occur was that the various parts of the curriculum, hung together without the bonding of theory, proved too difficult to assimilate during the short period of the course and, lacking reinforcement later, became difficult to build upon. Some respondents identifying a need to develop further their interpersonal skills cited management courses as the catalyst which enabled them to identify this need.

Other Comments from Respondents

There were other comments from respondents: three recorded that their lectures were presenting "red" political theories; four, that their lecturers discussed everything in terms of factory floor practices and did not relate anything to hospitals; one recorded that no one mentioned patients' needs throughout the course.

The high level of attendance at management educational courses suggests that when the educational concept becomes fashionable and Regional Health Authorities fund the programmes, local employing authorities will take advantage of the provision offered. It may be that if the same emphasis were given to other forms of educational programmes for nurses, the same high levels of attendance could be anticipated.

Satisfaction with Opportunities Available to Update Nursing Knowledge

A scale was devised to enable nurses to record their satisfaction with the facilities for updating nursing knowledge which they perceived to be available to them. This was Scale 2 and, as has already been stated of the scales developed for this research, the ordinal nature of the scaling was compensated for by using only scores of 25 or less to indicate dissatisfaction and scores above 75 to indicate satisfaction.

Forty-six per cent of respondents registered dissatisfaction and 8% registered satisfaction. Statistically significant differences were identified between the following groups: respondents on night duty, 59% of whom scored 25 or less; respondents on day duty, 42% of whom scored as dissatisfied; married nurses, 59% of whom scored 25 or less; unmarried nurses, 37% of whom scored 25 or less.

Home commitments also influenced results: of those with dependents 50% scored 25 or less while of those without dependents 41% scored as dissatisfied.

Specialties also had an effect: among midwives 16% were dissatisfied, while among others 51% were dissatisfied.

Grade also influenced in the general division: 21% of nursing officers scored 25 or less and 54% of charge nurses scored as dissatisfied.

Participants in post-basic educational programmes did not exhibit different responses overall but those who had participated in three or more programmes showed statistically significant differences from those who had not.

CHAPTER 6

Information on Other Means of Updating

6.1 Means Identified

Cooper (1970) discussed the means used by nurses to keep up to date with nursing and identified periodicals, books and experience, in addition to formal and informal educational programmes. However, MacGuire (1964) postulated that anti-intellectualism is incorporated into nurse training. It may be, of course, that "intellectual" is regarded in the same way as Smart (1972) told us that the adjective "academic" is regarded, when she stated that it is frequently used to mean "no good to man nor beast". In the National Health Service this view is suggested by other than nurses, since a research report on the care of the elderly (Cornell and Coles, 1979) recommended itself to an area health authority on the grounds that it was non-academic and, therefore, would be of use to decision makers. Anderson (1973) noted that nurses place great emphasis on experience as a means of increasing nursing knowledge and it is, perhaps, useful to remember that Rosen (1975) considered that:

"we are so utterly indoctrinated to believe that no true learning has taken place unless it has been written up or written out, that no one has seriously examined what kinds of important learning in any field might take place without a word having been written."

Accepting that this may appropriately be applied to nursing, it is interesting to examine, in the present study, the means indicated by respondents by which they keep up to date with nursing knowledge. Table 3 gives an overall view.

Accepting that means other than reading are available to nurses to enable them to keep up to date with nursing knowledge, it is worth recording that respondents also indicated an awareness of the value of reading material as a means of intellectual stimulus and as a source of professional knowledge and both written comments and the data from interviews suggested that respondents were aware of the paucity of easily available literature and viewed this as increasing the difficulty in keeping nursing knowledge up to date.

66

TABLE 3

Methods Recorded by Respondents as Available to Them to
Update Nursing Knowledge   N = 284

	%
Nursing journals	95
Formal training programmes	58
Consultants' rounds	52
Own resources	38
District study episodes	24
Informal discussion with medical staff	19
Lectures from medical staff	8
Information from professional associations	8
Nursing staff meetings	6
Contact with school of nursing	4
Use of post-graduate medical centre	2

By what Means do Nurses Update Nursing Knowledge?

Statistically significant differences were found to exist between:

1. Consultants' rounds which were mentioned by 66% of those qualified for less than 15 years and by 51% of those qualified for 15 years or more.
2. Own resources which were mentioned by 71% of nursing officers (general) and by 32% of charge nurses (general).
3. District study episodes which were mentioned by 26% of female respondents and by 10% of male respondents
4. Rcn/RCM/NATN Courses* which were mentioned by 33% of midwives, and by 4% of other groups.

It may be useful, at this point, to indicate the pedagogic nature of "consultants' rounds". Consultants in hospital tend to walk round the wards according to a set programme. The number in attendance can vary from the charge nurse only, to a group consisting of doctors of house officer and registrar grade (and in teaching hospitals, medical students) physiotherapists, and sometimes other nursing staff. A secretary may also attend. During such rounds patients are examined and diagnosed, treatment is prescribed, evaluated and changed. The condition of the patient is thus regularly monitored and decisions made based on information collected during these visits. The consultant concerned may discuss the aetiology of the disease, research findings regarding the treatment, the effect of drugs and the applicability of

* Royal College of Nursing, Royal College of Midwives, National Association of Theatres Nurses and like bodies.

investigations. The discussion may be joined by the charge nurse or it may be that she/he gives information only when asked. Other members of the group may also contribute. The discussion varies with the inclination and expertise of particular consultants from an in depth investigation of the condition of every patient to a rapid walk round to decide the next day's theatre list. No information was requested on the type of consultants' rounds in which respondents participated, only if they found it helpful in updating knowledge.

It is interesting that midwives recorded the Royal College of Midwives as a means by which more than one third of respondents keep professional knowledge up to date, but a very small proportion of general nurses regarded the Royal College of Nursing as such a source. Midwives recorded lectures and conferences attended both locally and further afield. No general nurse recorded local activity by the Rcn as a source of nursing updating.

One other category of programme not recorded with the above consists of three to five days inservice training described variously as: art of examining; art of teaching or art of teaching and examining. Thirty respondents, all of whom had attended other post basic programmes, recorded attendance at one of these courses. Since many nurses of nursing officer grade and even more of charge nurse grade act as examiners for the General Nursing Council's Assessments of nursing skills and acceptance as an examiner is dependent upon some such training, the small number of respondents recording attendance at such programmes was surprising. A small exercise was undertaken with a sample of charge nurses, all of whom were known to be examiners for the General Nursing Council for England and Wales. These nurses were outside the present research. It was found that of 20 nurses approached only one recalled the training programme related to examining when recording post-basic programmes attended. It may be that this situation operated with the sample of nurses approached for the purpose of this research. One charge nurse from the group approached outside the research stated when asked for some explanation—"You can hardly call three days a training programme."

6.2 Information on Journal Reading

The use of nursing journals as a means of keeping up to date with nursing presupposes that the information available is of use to nurses for this purpose and that all nursing journals are equally useful. This research asked only if nurses read nursing journals and 88% of respondents recorded reading a nursing journal in the month before the survey.

The literature suggests that nurses are subjected to an information explosion related to the expansion of hospital and other care services and the complexity of procedures for treatment which are being developed (Conley, 1972; Scott Wright, 1971 and Orr, 1979). Burns (1972) identified the American Journal of Nursing as a cheap method which offered help to nurses in their efforts to keep up to date. There is no similar study in this country relating to British nursing journals but it was assumed by the researcher that the reading of journals would be helpful rather than unhelpful to the nurse seeking information.

Availability of Nursing Journals

While 55% of respondents had nursing journals available in the hospital in which they worked, only 21% of respondents had journals conveniently available within the ward or department.

There were statistically significant differences between: those working in hospitals of 50 beds or less (73%) and others (50%).

Among those who had journals available within their working area significant differences were noted in the responses from: male nurses (9%) and female nurses (23%) and also between midwives—charge nurse grade (50%) and others (16%).

In general divisions differences were as follows: nursing officers 39% and charge nurses 13%.

Who Reads Nursing Journals?

Oppenheim (1966) reminds us of the difficulty of eliciting meaningful replies to questions of this kind since inaccuracies may creep in because of faulty recollection or because prestige bias may constrain people from answering accurately. Thus, while 95% of respondents recorded that they had read a nursing journal in the three months preceding the survey only 88% recorded reading a journal in the month before and this may be a more accurate record of reading habits. In an earlier study of the reading habits of trained nurses, Fisher and Strank (1971) recorded 86% of respondents as reading nursing journals. However, in that particular study the response rate of 23% could suggest an element of bias since those who responded might represent nurses who were interested in reading rather than all nurses.

In the present study there were statistically significant differences between male nurses (43%) and female nurses (64%) who recorded reading journals in the week before the study.

Of the journals recorded, the *Nursing Mirror* and the *Nursing Times* were by far the most frequently mentioned, 71% and 69% respectively. Eighteen per cent recorded the *British Medical Journal*. Only three respondents identified a non-British journal being available. Fourteen per cent of nursing officers and 4% of charge nurses recorded at least five journals as available.

Fifty-one per cent of respondents indicated that they bought nursing journals.

Again recalling Oppenheim (1966) who considers respondents may be reluctant to record negatively on a topic such as reading, it appeared reasonable to test the reliability of the response on reading journals by the response to the question "Who buys journals?" There is a negative correlation between the availability of nursing journals and the buying of them. Thus, those groups who have high proportions of journals available at work have low proportions buying nursing journals. In this respect statistically significant differences exist between: those qualified less than 15 years (62%) and those qualified 15 or more years (43%); while differences were also related to hospital size: those working in hospitals of 100 or more beds recorded 55% and those working in hospitals of less than 100 beds recorded 42%.

The social situation existing in smaller hospitals may explain some of this difference. In smaller hospitals staff tend to have a sitting room or other communal meeting place and the presence of journals in these rooms tends to make reading material more readily available to interested staff. In the larger hospitals journals tend to be available in: nursing libraries and central nursing offices. Such areas may be much less accessible to ward staff. Communal meeting places for nursing staff seem to be less available or less used in larger hospitals.

6.3 Use of Libraries

The General Nursing Council for England and Wales in a paper dated April 1980 stated that library services within the National Health Service should be regarded as essential for the provision of information in order to achieve high standards of patient care. Carmel (1975) suggested that there is a widespread disquiet about library services in the Health Services and dissatisfaction with existing standards and postulates a need for a library service which would be a clearing house for information and a resource centre distributing information/books/journals at appropriate points. He suggested a need for the rationalisation of all such services within a district, which seems in agreement with the General Nursing Council's (1980) expressed view that the library should offer a knowledge base for the practitioners of clinical services. Tabor (1979), considering library facilities for nurses, did not indicate that there has been much change in the thinking related to library provision for nurses. He saw this as essentially linked to the provision of library facilities for medical staff since nurses, he deduced, need some insight into the development of knowledge in medical and allied fields. Developments in these fields also have implications for nursing care and such knowledge is necessary for the

TABLE 4

Post-basic Programme Participants by Use of Facilities

Use of facilities	Participants	Non Participants	N	Sig.
Use of professional library:				
previous week	63%	37%	19	N.S.
previous month	67%	33%	30	diff 3 > S.E.
Use of other library (for profess. needs)				
previous year	56%	44%	100	N.S.
Read nursing journal previous week	59%	41%	174	diff 3 > S.E.
previous month	58%	42%	76	N.S.
Buy nursing journal	59%	41%	146	diff 3 S.E.
Read medical journal (in previous 3 months)	59%	41%	101	diff 3 μS.E.

nurse if the best possible care is to be available to patients. Thus he made a plea for the development of multidisciplinary health libraries in each health district. Tabor also identified libraries in the field of health care, as a support service for both clinical and management purposes which he recognised as being particularly important when the continuing educational needs of trained staff are being considered. Most of what he discussed was given some emphasis by respondents in the present research, either implicitly or explicitly.

Berg (1973) noted the participants in education programmes made more use of journals and libraries than did non-participants and this was examined in the present study. Table 4 shows that there is some support for this in the findings of the present research. Bergman (1979) in a study relating to nurses of similar grade to charge nurses in Israel, noted that nurses who participated in post basic educational programmes exhibited greater satisfaction with available facilities than did non-participants.

Who Uses Libraries?

Fifty-four per cent of respondents indicated that they used libraries. However, this was in the year previous to the survey and related to the use of a professional library within the employing health district. When this was related to the period just before the survey the following percentages occurred: in the month previous to the survey 11% and in the week previous to the survey 7%.

There is little evidence in the present research that trained nurses are frequent users of libraries. Some explanation for this may be found in Carmel's (1975) paper already referred to where he suggested that libraries in the health service are not necessarily suited to potential users. Some comments from respondents in the present survey indicated that this may be so and the following examples were recorded:

"It is six miles to the school of nursing where the library is."
"The library is always closed when I can use it."
"I don't think they like sisters using the library."
"When I have finished work the last thing I think of trying to find is a library."

Twelve per cent of respondents found that the libraries available met all their needs; 48% of these (16) had not used a library in the year previous to the survey. Nineteen per cent of respondents found that the libraries available met none of their needs. Statistically significant differences among users were found between: respondents from hospitals of 200 beds or more (65%) and respondents from hospitals of less than this (44%). This may to some extent be explained by the fact the nursing libraries are usually associated with schools of nursing and are most likely to be attached to larger hospitals, indicating that when facilities are available within easy reach of ward staff they are more likely to be used.

The following differences were indicated between general division nursing officers of whom 71% had used a library in the year previous to the survey and charge nurses of whom 51% had used a library in the same period.

Thirty-five per cent of respondents had used a general public library for health service purposes in the year previous to the survey. There were no statistically significant differences between the groups.

Because nursing practice is influenced by changes in medical thinking and new knowledge in medicine has implications for nursing (Chapman, 1977; McFarlane, 1976; Castledine, 1977) the extent to which nurses avail themselves of information from medical journals was sought, and 82% of respondents considered that nurses should read medical journals but only 36% of respondents had read such a journal in the three months before the survey. Of those who had read a medical journal in the month before the survey (15%), significant differences existed between: those working in specialty areas (24%) this group included midwives and those working in other areas (10%).

There were comments from some staff in specialist units indicating that access to medical journals occurred because doctors brought journals to the unit. Specialist units (including midwifery) also frequently have libraries. These are small but accessible to staff.

Three comments were made by those who did not consider that nurses should read medical journals. These were:

"These journals are too high powered for nurses."
"You can only understand bits of them."
"I can barely find time to read nursing journals."

Who is Satisfied with Journal and Library Facilities?

A scale was devised to measure respondents' level of satisfaction with the facilities available. (Chapter 4). Forty per cent of respondents scored 25 or less and those who scored in this part of the scale were categorised as dissatisfied. Statistically significant differences existed between nursing officers (20%) and charge nurses (43%) and also between male nurses (57%) and female nurses (38%).

The influence of other variables was apparent: of those who had journals in hospital 33% registered dissatisfaction; of those who did not have journals in hospital 46% were dissatisfied; of those who had journals in ward/department 20% were dissatisfied; of those who did not have journals in ward/department 50% were dissatisfied.

Other differences occurred as follows: of those who had read medical journals 33% were dissatisfied; of those who had not read medical journals 45% were dissatisfied; of those who found professional libraries useful 26% were dissatisfied; of those who did not find professional libraries useful 69% were dissatisfied. Thirty-eight per cent of participants in post-basic programmes were dissatisfied, and 44% of non participants were dissatisfied.

Of those who scored in the satisfied area of the scale (above 75) 70% were participants in post-basic educational programmes.

It is apparent that nurses' needs for professional updating by means of libraries and journals are not being met by the facilities available. It is also implied by comments made by some respondents that libraries in the health services were viewed as repositories of text books only and not as an information resource facility. Respondents were also aware that libraries in schools of nursing were, not unnaturally, designed for the use of learner nurses and not those of trained staff. Few respondents were aware of other professional library facilities. Indeed, at the time of the survey, other facilities were limited, post-graduate medical centre libraries being used in the main exclusively by medical staff*.

Other libraries available to nurses in the region are London based, for example, King's Fund Centre Library and the Royal College of Midwives Library. Such libraries are not easily accessible to nurses working full-time and running homes for families. There is, therefore, a

---

* This has now changed; the post graduate medical centre libraries are now available to all trained health service staff and some are being stocked accordingly.

73

need for easier access if libraries are to fulfil the aim expressed by the General Nursing Council (1980) that the library service offers a "knowledge base" to ensure that management decisions are made in the light of relevant knowledge and is the natural focus of research based practice.

Gillespie (1978) in a letter to the *Nursing Times* suggests that in Scotland, where library provision is adequate, there is evidence that nurses make good use of the facility.

6.4 Regression Analysis of Significant Variables

The sub-programme Multiple Regression was used to identify variables which predicted levels of satisfaction with facilities recorded on Scales 1 and 2. The variables included were those which showed significant differences in the scores of certain categories of respondents.

Scale 1

Variables

1. Sex of respondents
2. Shifts worked
3. Grade of nurse
4. Availability of journals:
   in hospital
   in work place

5. Attendance at post-basic educational programme (including all three categories)
6. Social status
7. Presence of dependents
8. Type of nursing (general/maternity)

The results of this analysis were disappointing in that only 17% of the variance could be accounted for by the variables entered. The influencing variables were: Availability of journals; grade of nurse; sex of respondent; reading of medical journals and attendence at post-basic educational programmes.

It can be seen that 7% of the variance can be accounted for by the presence of journals in the workplace. The other variables accounted for the remaining 10% of variance. This suggests that a variety of journals circulating through wards and departments, perhaps on a unit basis, would enable nurses to achieve higher levels of satisfaction with facilities available.

Scale 2

Variables

1. Sex of respondents
2. Shift worked
3. Grade of nurse

4. Availability of journals:
   in work place
   in hospital

74

5. Reading of medical journals
6. Attendance at post-basic programmes (including all three categories)
7. Social status
8. Dependents
9. Type of nursing

Twenty-one per cent of the variance can be accounted for by the variable entered and 17% of the variance can be influenced by one variable only. Thus:

Presence of dependents	17%
Type of nursing	1%
Grade of nurse	1%
Sex of respondents	1%
Shift worked	
Availability of journals	
Social status	1%
Reading of medical journals	
Attendance at post-basic education programmes (all three categories)	

This suggests that the presence of dependents among nursing staff has a strong influence on the acceptability of educational courses available to them and since 45% of respondents in the sample recorded that they had dependents, the planning of such programmes must take cognisance of this.

CHAPTER 7

Other Information Collected

7.1 Final Comments Examined

In order to make the utmost use of the data available, the final comments supplied by respondents were investigated using the process of content analysis. Lindzey and Aronson (1954) stated that, when using this process, categories may be identified by means of a preliminary impressionistic analysis and Galtung (1967) said that these categories must be treated in the same way as other units of analysis. In this research the categories were identified from the unstructured final comments of respondents and the analysis yielded 10 classes of response; nine specific and one generalised category containing miscellaneous entries. Ninety-eight respondents (35%) made 185 comments. Six comments related to the respondents' interest in the questionnaire and have been abstracted from the rest of the analysis, leaving 177 comments.

Categories of Comments

Category 1
A need for new knowledge to enable trained nurses to keep up to date with nursing.
Fifty-one respondents referred to this—29% of comments. This was 18% of all respondents.

Category 2
An expressed awareness of discouragement from the organisation for whom they worked, in their efforts to keep up to date with new knowledge.
Thirty-one respondents referred to this—18% of comments. This was 11% of all respondents.

Category 3
A need for a new flexible approach to continuing nursing education. Here the use of films, cassettes and postal courses were mentioned.
Twenty-eight respondents referred to this—16% of comments. This was 10% of all respondents.

Category 4
A need for publicity regarding locally available programmes.
Twelve respondents referred to this—7% of comments. This was 4% of all respondents

Category 5
A need for library facilities at times when the library can be used.
Twelve respondents referred to this—7% of comments. This was 4% of all respondents

Category 6
A need for compulsory updating programmes.
Twelve respondents referred to this—7% of comments. This was 4% of all respondents

Category 7
A need for more appropriate management training.
Ten respondents referred to this—6% of comments. This was 3% of all respondents.

Category 8
A need for effective programmes to give some skill in teaching nurses on the ward.
Eight respondents referred to this—4% of comments. This was 3% of all respondents.

Category 9
An identification of post basic up-dating programmes being used as a "reward" rather than as a necessary part of staff development.
Six respondents referred to this—3% of comments. This was 2% of all respondents.
Percentages are rounded, where appropriate. Such percentages become less valid as numbers diminish.

Category 10
This group contained responses from:
Three charge nurses who kept up to date with nursing by reading nursing journals.
Two charge nurses who kept up to date with nursing by talking to doctors.
Two charge nurses who stated that trained nurses should keep up to date with nursing by nursing patients and not by going on courses.

The opportunity to utilise a different technique for data gathering, within the framework of an otherwise rather tightly structured questionnaire is useful and this self-generated data enriched the research and content analysis enabled such data to be disciplined into identifiable categories.

TABLE 5
Categories of Comments Related to Percentage of Comments and of
Respondents

Category	% of Comments	% of Respondents
1	29% (51)	18%
2	18% (31)	11%
3	16% (28)	10%
4	7% (12)	4%
5	7% (12)	4%
6	7% (12)	4%
7	6% (10)	3%
8	4% (8)	3%
9	3% (6)	2%

(Figures in brackets represent numbers of comments)

7.2 Data From Interviews

Webb (1977) suggested that different data gathering techniques applied to the same problem help to clarify response. In the present research, triangulation was attempted by means of the following approaches:

1. The use of a questionnaire.
2. The content analysis of final comments in the questionnaire.
3. The use of data from interviews.

Benney and Hughes (1956) considered that by its very nature the interview is a transitory experience and noted that it is essential to establish a reciprocatory relationship in the short time available; therefore, an interview, which is a meeting with a purpose, is dependent upon interaction between the people involved. Benney, Reisman and Starr (1956) reminded us that the interviewer takes certain attributes to the interview and commented on the influence that factors such as age, sex or ethnic group may have upon the data collected. Williams (1970) also concluded that interviewer role performance is a factor influencing response. These views were useful reminders of the difficulty of developing absolute neutrality when conducting interviews. The attempts made by the researcher to reduce any potential tensions associated with the interview are described in Chapter 4. The experience of Davies (1971) in initiating interviews with charge nurses was also an influence. Charge nurses to whom questionnaires were being distributed (those who were selected for interview) were asked to participate in an interview and the time was set as soon as was convenient for the charge nurse. Most appointments were made for the afternoon of that day and all appointments were kept, the researcher stating that if the ward situation altered and the work pressures were too great at the time arranged a new appointment would be made. In fact, although some interviews were delayed no interviews were cancelled.

As already described the interview setting varied according to the local situation and the researcher concentrated on achieving a period free from interruption, in an environment which enabled a relaxed discussion to take place. The weather was dry and warm and the gardens were often used when there were secluded areas with seats available.

Appendix E shows the check list used to guide the interview. The questionnaire already distributed was also ultilised in the initial stages of each interview to identify the priority given to the items included (Table 6).

TABLE 6
Priority Given to Items in Section 1

Priority	Item
1.	Need for adequate nursing library
2.	Need for journals in an accessible place
3.	Need for small specialist ward library
4.	Adequate selection of journals
5.	Journals available in workplace
6.	Library opening hours to suit users

The responses here reflected the respondents' perception of what was available. Some respondents referred to the inaccessibility of libraries and some to the libraries being designed for learner nurses and, therefore, that trained nurses were not appropriate users. The following statement demonstrates this:

"I have the feeling that I should not borrow anything although they don't mind my reading in the library."

Hospitals in some districts were very scattered and this was indicated by some respondents as a reason for difficulty in taking advantage of district library facilities which were known to be available. Financial difficulties facing the National Health Service were regarded by many respondents as a limitation on any funds which could legitimately be made available for the dispersion of books/journals throughout hospitals.

Comments regarding journals included these aspects:
Journals were available in some hospitals and in small hospitals were readily available in sitting rooms or dining areas.

79

Journals were available in school of nursing libraries.
Journals were available but in stituations such as the waiting areas around nursing administrative offices.

The researcher was able to observe that this was indeed the case. Many hospitals had, freely available, in waiting areas attached to nursing administrative offices collections of one or more nursing journals. However, as Davies (1971) noted the complexities of the status hierarchies in nursing may militate against the utilisation of journals in these circumstances and it was evident from discussion with charge nurses that journals, available as described, were not considered to be easily accessible as reference material. There were subtleties here which were not explored fully. Charge nurses interviewed considered that nursing journals were a means of keeping up to date with nursing but several respondents suggested that leaving the ward to look up information in journals would not be considered appropriate behaviour.

Nursing officers, on the other hand, expressed the views that journals were available to all trained staff and none of those interviewed considered that the siting of these journals in administrative office suites would inhibit their use by ward staff.

The need for appropriate text books to be available in the wards was mentioned by several charge nurses, some of whom used their own books in this way. Many of these described their text books as out of date. One charge nurse stated that she tried to add one such book regularly and estimated that she contributed books every couple of years.

There were few nurses who recorded a wide selection of journals being available. Seventy-nine per cent of respondents recorded one to five journals available. Some respondents used the post-graduate medical centre library, stating that it was easy to get permission and that the selection of journals was wide. Again, only those working in hospitals designated as district general hospitals mentioned this. The percentage of nursing officers who perceived a wider selection of journals being available to them was 14% and charge nurses 8%. This difference may reflect the difference in role which exists, since charge nurses, as Davies (1971) described are ward-centred and, therefore, may perceive availability strictly in ward terms, whereas nursing officers by definition are unit based and a unit may be dispersed geographically, allowing the nursing officer access to facilities over a wider area and, therefore, increasing awareness.

At interview some charge nurses also mentioned making their own journals available to staff within their wards. Others (three) mentioned medical journals being left by doctors. However, these were not available on a systematic basis.

That the nurses interviewed saw a need for updating information to be available to aid professional development was well supported by the interview findings. Respondents were also well aware of the financial implications of such facilities. There was some conflict as to the justification for spending more funds and the lack of reality associated with such expectations was mentioned by several charge nurses, who indicated that when budgets were tight, as they perceived them to be, it was unrealistic to think that such expenditure would be made. Several charge nurses indicated that their local authority libraries were helpful in obtaining professional material.

The next area which was discussed was clinical updating relating to education programmes (Table 7).

TABLE 7
Priority Given to Items in Section 2

Priority	Type of Programme
1 & 2	District based clinical programmes
3.	Need for specialist updating
4.	Need for more formal training programmes
5.	Better organised local lecture programmes
6.	Series of local study days covering one topic

It is appreciated that it is unrealistic to expect nurses, who are not educationists to identify specific training/educational methods and what was hoped here was that those interviewed would be able to indicate deficits. It was evident from responses that nurses were thinking in very traditional terms when they considered any updating methods.

MacGuire (1964) has indicated the narrow professional basis of nurse training and it is a weakness in the present study that no particular effort was made to probe the views of respondents regarding the effect of this on their performance as charge nurses. Certainly, from the information offered it was apparent that nurses were well aware of the essential nature of interpersonal skills related to the charge nurse role but only two charge nurses stated specifically that they felt a lack of such training in their nursing education.

There was a consensus view among those interviewed that updating programmes for trained nurses should be available locally. Most nurses considered that the additional burden of having to leave their home district would reduce interest in such programmes if they were available.

Subsequent data relate to the information detailed in the Check List (see Appendix E).

The attitude of the employing authorities towards the needs of respondents to update nursing knowledge was sought. If this was not mentioned spontaneously it was asked if those being interviewed considered:

a. They were encouraged to take advantage of updating opportunities?
b. Their ability to do this was taken for granted?
c. There was indifference to their ability to do this?
d. They perceived themselves as being discouraged from doing this?

It was interesting that almost all respondents considered the financial implications of updating programmes and this constraint was offered by some as an explanation for lack of encouragement. In addition, many charge nurses stated that it was relatively easy to get funds if further education were needed to train as a teacher of nurses but that further education in clinical matters (if it lasted longer than one day) was regarded as a luxury in relation to clinical nurses (Table 8).

TABLE 8
Attitudes to Updating

Responses	Numbers
Positively discouraged	8
Not discouraged but little available	7
Not discouraged but no money available	7
Updating taken for granted	5
Encouraged	4
Total	31

In addition to these comments, some charge nurses in the general divisions also commented that attendance at any kind of educational programme was presented by way of reward, rather than as a necessary commitment to competence. Two nursing officers interviewed, on the other hand, considered that charge nurses "expected everything to be handed to them on a plate".

Several nurses discussed this topic in terms of "professional" updating. This clearly meant that they were seeking knowledge relating to nursing and did not necessarily imply a sociological definition of professionalism. However, this awareness of a body of knowledge necessary to nursing may be an indication that nurses are, as Fretwell (1980) stated, in a developmental state regarding professionalism.

It is perhaps useful here to remember that, because of the interviewing format used, it was not possible to maintain a set method of questioning nor to use pre-determined probes to elicit information.

The interviewer did, however, endeavour to maintain a neutral attitude and most probing took the form of "Could you explain that a little" or "Am I interpreting you correctly?" At the end of each interview the interviewer read to the respondent what she had recorded and amended any mis-interpretations.

When the question of updating needs and the related potential for reducing the time spent with patients was pursued charge nurses in the general division expressed the following views:

a. Keeping up to date with nursing did not reduce the time spent with patients because it had to take place in the periods out of working hours.

b. Time spent in improving knowledge is of benefit to patients because it results in better care.

Midwifery staff stated that the time spent in updating and increasing knowledge was a necessary part of a midwife's career. Patients were more likely to be well looked after if the midwife was confident and knowledgeable midwives were more likely to be confident.

Nursing officers all stated that they felt that the investment of time was not to the detriment of patient care. This was referring to their own needs and one nursing officer considered that more training was needed in management techniques but that this was actively encouraged where she worked. Four of the nursing officers interviewed did not consider that they had opportunity for systematic updating. One considered that the present management training available within the National Health Service was systematic and adequate.

All midwifery staff regarded their opportunities for systematic updating to be adequate.

Charge nurses in the general divisions responded differently. There was general agreement that there was no opportunity for systematic updating. One charge nurse who had attended a Joint Board of Clinical Nursing Studies course just before her appointment to her post a few months before the survey said that she felt that she was happy about her own opportunities but she did not know what others did. Two main points were made: those who took time and trouble were unacknowledged; those who made no effort were regarded as being just as competent as those who did try to keep up to date.

This evidence of a need for effort to be rewarded, either by being recognised by seniors or in terms of promotion, was also noted by Berg (1973) in an American study. No charge nurse interviewed regarded local study episodes as offering opportunity of systematic updating. However, in one health district the post-basic department of the school of nursing considered that they provided the opportunity for charge nurses to devise ways of meeting their own updating needs in a systematic manner by offering them the possibility of taking part in any programme available whether for learners or trained nurses. No nurse interviewed in that district indicated any awareness of such opportunities.

When the data for this research were collected the effects of the 1974 reorganisation of the National Health Service were still being felt and respondents expressed the following views on this: management changes of this kind had little impact on nurses working in the wards. More than two thirds of respondents indicated this. A few nurses stated that decision making took very much longer. Another small group considered that the reorganisation had brought great benefits to the hospital.

Varying views were expressed regarding the nursing management structure operating. Most nurses considered that the management pattern developed after the publication of the Salmon Report (1966) had resulted in benefits for the charge nurse which enabled her/him to concentrate on the delivery of care to the patient within the wards. However, some charge nurses recognised their relationship with nursing officers as being part of a social exchange (Chapman, 1977). These charge nurses viewed themselves as risking a loss of autonomy in clinical decision making in exchange for a reduction in administrative work. One charge nurse explained, "It takes away some of the irritating interruptions but you pay a price in interference at ward level."

Career Prospects

These were considered by most of those interviewed to have improved considerably but about half of the charge nurses qualified this by saying that opportunities for higher salaries had improved but not for nurses who wanted to remain looking after patients. All nursing officers felt that career opportunities were improved.

The Role of the Clinical Nurse Consultant

One other area of information was investigated. Nursing literature since 1970 has contained many references to the role of the clinical nurse consultant. The Royal College of Nursing Paper (1974) describes the training for such a role and gives some descriptive definitions of its operation. In describing the post to the nurses interviewed, care was taken to differentiate this from the role of clinical specialist, usually a nursing officer, operating in a specialty field, for example, the nurse in charge of a renal dialysis unit. The role was defined as that of a nurse with clinical expertise who would be available to the charge nurse for consultation on clinical nursing problems. It was suggested that this expertise would be based on experience enhanced by advanced education. The education needed was not specified. Two charge nurses considered that this might be an interesting development allowing patient-orientated nurses to remain in touch with patient care. However, both these nurses were sceptical of the ability of such nurses to maintain clinical expertise and both considered that the role would be in conflict with medical consultants, who would resent the development and create difficulties for an incumbent. They considered, also, that nurses in senior management posts would likewise see the role as threatening. All other charge nurses considered that this development could only be harmful to nurses in charge of wards. It was clearly stated by these nurses that clinical expertise should be available at ward level and that nurses of charge nurse grade were the people who needed this and should be encouraged to acquire and maintain this expertise.

No midwife saw the role as a reality, citing the need for practitioners to be experts in the practice of midwifery.

Nursing officers responded differently. All but one of the nursing officers considered that the role described was the one that they enacted. Some of these nurses had available their job descriptions which described the nursing officer as a clinical expert (these job descriptions were based on those examples given in the Salmon Report, 1966). The responses suggested that this potential development was seen as a threat to status and described as likely to create difficulties for the nurse in the ward and for nursing officers.

All the charge nurses interviewed described the nursing officer as an "enabler" who was needed to clear the way for the charge nurse so that she/he could concentrate on the organisation of patient care. No charge nurse reported that the nursing officer operated as a clinical expert.

In Chapter 1 the literature was examined to clarify understanding of the concept of role and the development of conflict both within and between roles. It was apparent from the interviews undertaken that although sociological terminology was not used, the nurses interviewed had considerable understanding of the concept and also had awareness of potential areas of conflict. Charge nurses saw the difficulties experienced by nursing officers whose awareness of the needs, for example, for adequate staffing levels, was difficult to reconcile with management policies operating. Role boundaries were clearly recognised—charge nurses differentiating between the nursing officer's control of resources and the charge nurses' control over the organisation of the services within the ward. One nursing officer also discussed role stress which she recognised at senior officer level and commented that:

"She (the senior nursing officer) cannot go on fighting for resources for us as she does; it makes her job impossible. No one seems to be able to understand the need of nurses for educational opportunities."

Professional development was also acknowledged as a requirement, one charge nurse stating that nurses in charge of wards stagnate if they

85

do not have the opportunity to acquire information on developments in nursing. Pembrey (1980) in discussion with charge nurses stated that not only did charge nurses need access to new knowledge in nursing but also needed to have the means of assuring themselves that their knowledge was current. This seemed also to be identified by the nurses who were interviewed for this research.

7.3 Other Interviews

In order to establish the degree to which updating, post-basic education was available to nurses, interviews were sought with those who provided educational programmes for nurses and in addition to personnel in schools of nursing, representatives from other institutions responsible for the education of trained nurses were arranged. These included the Royal College of Nursing, Joint Board of Clinical Nursing Studies, two universities and a polytechnic. In schools of nursing in the districts included in the sample, three schools had a tutor responsible for post-basic/in-service education in post for several years previous to the survey. One school made such an appointment during the survey and the other two districts made such an appointment later. Respondents from hospitals in these districts who worked in hospitals peripheral to the district general hospital were not always aware that there was such a person in post in the district, suggesting that existing communication systems were not always successful, although one district reported that all educational sessions were advertised on prominent notice boards and were identified by brightly coloured notices. This, however, makes the assumption that the target population looks at the notice board. The type of programme available in the districts which had a tutor in post, varied considerably. The main thrust in one district was through courses approved by the Joint Board of Clinical Nursing Studies, while at the same time offering study days to charge nurses and other trained nurses covering a variety of topics. In this district also the department was prepared to offer study facilities to any charge nurse who identified a particular need, utilising any programme being provided by the school of nursing. This flexible approach was recognised by some nurses in the district general hospital but staff in other hospitals in the district were not so well informed. Another district offered a variety of study days for trained staff and provided these on a hierarchical basis which meant that similar programmes were repeated for several grades of trained nurses, resulting in nurses being eligible to attend programmes every few months. Topics included lectures on fire prevention in a programme which also has a lecture on the behavioural sciences. Another programme was devoted to alcoholism. In this school most sessions were part of a working day, the other sessions taking all of a working day. A third district in the year before the survey offered 13 sessions to trained nurses, for example, surgical dressing techniques, care of the dying, and legal aspects of nursing. This district also provided art of examining programmes and had an affiliation with a college of education which provided training in teaching techniques on a half-day release basis for ten weeks. In the year previous to the survey 12 people had attended. In these districts the programmes provided were based on needs identified by the providers from information acquired from staff within the health districts. No particular pattern was identified in the provision nor was there any evidence of follow-up or reinforcement of the information presented. Nurses who were responsible for educational programmes for trained nurses were also responsible for the provision of inservice training for nursing auxiliaries, which may have encroached upon the time available for the planning and development of programmes for trained nurses. It must also be noted that management education was the responsibility of another educational system organised by the training division of the regional health authority.

Health districts without tutors specialising in post-basic educational programmes, at the time of the survey, offered the same *ad hoc* approach to the updating of nursing knowledge but even less systematically and fewer study days were available. Interestingly, in all health districts all staff reported a study session devoted to the change to an international system of measurement within the National Health Service. This change had been occurring at different rates in different sections of the service over several years and the period of the survey marked the end of the changeover. In an interview with personnel at the Hendon Police College, staff concerned with the ongoing training of experienced police officers, stated that while it was difficult to plan programmes for police officers which would generally update personnel, all areas responded immediately to the production of programmes devoted to riot control techniques. Perhaps the Système International represents for nurses the concrete area of change that riot control represents for the police. This of course stresses the importance of noting what changes are occurring and sharing this perception with nurses themselves, in order to plan programmes which meet expectations. Certainly the responses of charge nurses indicated that what is offered locally, while it may be interesting, is unsatisfactory in enabling nurses to feel confident that they are maintaining their competence and increasing knowledge. It is worth remembering that Luck *et al* (1971) writing of patients, hospitals and operational research, said of the charge nurse that she/he has a large amount of discretion in the organisation of patient care which thus affects the treatment and care that patients receive. It is this importance of the charge nurse role which creates the need for emphasis on the ability of charge nurses to maintain competence by means of educational updating, in addition to empirical extension of knowledge.

As previously noted responses indicated awareness of certain biases existing in the support given to nurses pursuing advanced nursing education. Interviews with staff from the two universities offering advanced nursing education with a clinical option confirmed this to some degree. Personnel from both Edinburgh and Manchester noted that nurses who chose the clinical programmes (leading to a master of science degree) were mostly self financing or from overseas. In Leeds, where an extension programme leads to a first degree for trained nurses, it was also reported that applicants were having difficulty in raising financial support. At the time of the survey these three institutions were providing the only courses available to nurses at an advanced academic level and the Leeds programme was in the planning stage at the time of the survey. It is thus apparent that there is little choice available to nurses when seeking such education and the leaning towards locally produced programmes may well be influenced by the distance from home of the courses available.

It is necessary now to discuss the London University Diploma in Nursing course which is available in many centres throughout the country. Only 4% of respondents recorded this programme as a means of updating or increasing nursing knowledge. Interviews could not be arranged with staff from the university but a letter published in a nursing journal (Burtt-Jones, 1980) stated that this course registered 4,027 students for 1976–77. There has been no opportunity to identify why this discrepancy exists and interviews with charge nurses indicated that while respondents were aware of the existence of the courses they seemed to view them as largely irrelevant. The absence of information from the university makes it difficult to draw any conclusions from this information.

It has been stated that respondents were knowledgeable about the provision of specialist education in nursing (for example the Joint Board of Clinical Nursing Studies) and recognised the value of these courses in developing skills in specialties. The programmes provided were not designed to update knowledge in the specialties in which training is provided and although the gap which exists in the provision of updating programmes for general nurses was acknowledged, the present terms of reference of the Board do not encompass this aspect of nursing education.

An interview with a representative of the Royal College of Nursing, at the London headquarters, indicated that its advanced nursing, educational programmes concentrated mainly on teacher training courses and on education in management and administration. Certain specialty areas, such as occupational health are also catered for. In addition to these, Diploma in Nursing programmes are available. Nurses in clinical practice are helped by assistance in the development of associations for those with certain special needs, for example, those working in renal dialysis units and assistance is given in the organising of conferences etc., for these self-help groups, while it acts as a facilitator in the development of the associations.

In examining the facilities available to trained nurses for educational development, the respondents' lack of awareness of much opportunity reflects the reality. There is a lack of co-ordination in what is made available and little new thinking in what needs to be provided. The useful libraries available in London are not helpful to nurses in other areas and the library facilities available in the health districts through the post-graduate medical centres are designed to meet medical rather than nursing needs. The two streams of education available, management and clinical, are organised independently of each other and no common core is identified and built upon. However, the social science basis of management courses could be useful in extending knowledge in other areas of nursing and could be used to meet criteria which still need to be developed, so that educational programmes can be evaluated as part of an ongoing system of nursing education.

7.4 Some Other Information Recorded

Basic Nursing Training—was this Sufficient to Equip Respondents for their Present Role?

This question produced replies which were surprising in view of other information offered. Fifty-four per cent answered "Yes". Statistically significant differences existed between: those qualified less than 15 years, 43% of whom recorded this and those qualified 15 or more years, 62% of whom recorded "Yes"; respondents from hospitals of less than 100 beds 75% of whom recorded "Yes"; respondents from hospitals of 100 or more beds 45% of whom recorded "Yes".

Most respondents who considered that their basic training was sufficient to enable them to undertake their present post commented either:

a. That they had trained at a time when basic training was considerably better than the training being presently offered;
b. That they had trained at a training school which offered very much better training than was available in most hospitals.

Only some respondents recorded training at teaching hospitals. It is possible that in replying to this qestion respondents were conscious of loyalties to an alma mater and considered that negative replies implied unjustified criticism of the training school. McGuire (1964) discussed this and suggested that this loyalty to hospital, inculcated during the training period, includes a denial of the right to criticise. The design of the survey did not allow this subject to be pursued and it is an interesting area for further exploration. It would be useful to know, for example, why nursing officers considered that basic training equipped them sufficiently since no respondents in the survey in nursing officer posts could have trained at a time when such posts existed. Also it could be asked: What difference does hospital size make? Are changes in practice less evident in hospitals of less than 100 beds?

It was asked of respondents if they saw a need for short updating courses from which they could choose a programme to meet their own individual needs. Ninety-seven per cent of respondents saw a need for this.

There was some divergence of view as to whether such updating should be voluntary or compulsory. Among the 97% who recorded a need 71% considered that such updating should be voluntary. Twenty-eight per cent felt that this should be compulsory. Statistically significant differences existed only between: those working in general areas, 77% of whom preferred voluntary attendance; those working in specialised areas (this includes midwifery), 63% of whom preferred voluntary attendance. This point also demonstrated the view of respondents regarding systematic updating such as that which is mandatory for midwives. Overall 3% of respondents considered that this was unnecessary. Statistically significant differences existed between the views of respondents regarding whether or not such updating should be compulsory: 84% of midwives recorded that it should be while 53% of others also recorded that it should be, 58% of respondents considered that there should be a systematic updating on a compulsory basis.

Other factors which may be of importance to nurses when they are considering the need for updating nursing knowledge include:

1. Potential mobility
2. Preferred time span
3. Preference for full time or part time study

Who is Free to Travel?

Only 19% of respondents recorded an ability to travel away from the home district. Statistically significant differences existed between: married respondents, 13% of whom could travel and unmarried respondents, 29% of whom could travel; those who worked full time, 23% of whom could travel and those who worked part time, 5% of whom could travel.

This may be demonstrating that career orientated respondents (those who work full time and are unmarried) can devote more time to the updating of nursing knowledge than can other staff. It must be remembered, however, that all of the respondents in this study are in charge of wards and departments for some part of the working day or night and will need to be as well informed as any other nurse who is in charge.

90

How Long Should a Programme Last?

More than half of the respondents (79%) preferred study programmes lasting no more than one week and only 10% considered attendances at courses of longer than one month. Thirty-five per cent recorded a willingness to use their own time to keep up to date with nursing. There were no statistically significant differences between groups.

Part Time rather than Full Time Study?

In this research part time study is defined as study undertaken while still responsible for a ward or department. This means day release or some similar arrangement or study undertaken outside working hours. Forty-one per cent of all respondents preferred this. Statistically significant differences existed regarding preference for part time study between those working on night duty (54%) and those working on day duty (38%) and those qualified 25 or more years, (57%) and others (36%); and those working in specialty areas, (57%) and others (39%).

Who could Extend the Working Day to Include Study/Travel?

Overall, 50% of respondents could thus extend the working day. Statistically significant differences existed between: nursing officers (72%) and charge nurses (49%).

One other group which showed statistically significant differences included those working at nights, 61% of whom could not extend the working day and those working on day duty, 45% of whom could not extend the working day.

CHAPTER 8

Discussion and Conclusions

In recording the way nurses use libraries, it is apparent from this study that the libraries at the disposal of trained nurses are neither conveniently available to them nor do they contain material which is necessarily useful. Indeed, for many respondents their right to adequate library facilities was a somewhat unexpected concept. There is a need for nurses to be made aware of the valuable nursing writings now being published and where these are available. Research on topics of interest to nurses working in wards needs to be brought to the attention of such nurses in a systematic way. Seminars/discussions would enable this to occur. There is no evidence from respondents in the study that such opportunities are available. Such seminars could form part of an educational pattern which would allow discussion to develop around the topics being highlighted in journals etc., since without such opportunities charge nurses are somewhat isolated within their own departments and have little outlet for exchanging views with their peers. From the information supplied on journal reading, it can be seen that the range of journals within reach of these nurses was very limited. Most respondents referred only to the *Nursing Mirror* and the *Nursing Times.* Medical journals, such as the *British Medical Journal, The Lancet* and *Modern Geriatrics,* were recorded as being available by about 20% of respondents. A further 2% mentioned other journals. Little reference was made to material published overseas. The recognition of the similarities of nursing problems existing in other countries, despite the differences in the organisation of nursing services and training, could be of value to nurses. Other perspectives, which contribute to new thinking, could lead to new solutions to old problems. The existing provision of reading material for trained nurses is of minimal usefulness in reaching the nurses in charge of wards and there is little incentive, at present, for nurses to make the considerable effort needed to overcome this. The number of nurses using public libraries for professional purposes indicates that the inconvenience/inadequacy of hospital libraries at district level does act as a constraint upon their use.

Without knowledge shared among nurses by means of journals and other published material and opportunities to discuss and evaluate such new knowledge, it is difficult for this to be disseminated and assimilated. This research shows that, at present, there is little evidence that opportunities of this kind exist. The scores on Scale 1 which record satisfaction with such facilities suggests that there is an awareness among respondents that a more systematic approach to the problem is needed.

Moving on to other processes by which trained nurses keep up to date with new knowledge, 58% of respondents had attended some formal post-basic training programme, and on the whole were well informed regarding the Joint Board of Clinical Nursing Studies courses available. There was, however, a clear understanding of the financial implications associated with other types of educational programmes and charge nurses stated, at interview, that unless nurses were interested in acquiring a teaching qualification, it was virtually impossible to be considered for any advanced nursing educational programme. This was borne out by comments made by educationists in Edinburgh, Manchester and Leeds, where it was stated that students taking clinical or research options in the programmes offered, were, in the main, self-financed, while those attending teaching options were seconded. It is appreciated that only a small proportion of charge nurses will be interested in the educational programmes offered by the universities. However, the newer developments of extension programmes offered by polytechnics, which enable nurses to build on their basic education and undertake studies leading to a first degree, will offer greater opportunities in the future. If, however, the official indifference recognised in relation to programmes already available persists, the effort needed by nurses to overcome this resistance, in addition to the efforts needed to undertake additional studies may prove too difficult. The Diploma of Nursing programmes also could be used as a means of offering educational development to nurses seeking promotion to charge nurse grade, presuming that they could be organised to meet this need.

When the data were collected for the present research only the universities of Manchester and Edinburgh were offering advanced nursing education with a clinical option. In addition to this, management studies at advanced level are available at several universities and polytechnics and there is a course in social research with a health service option at the University of Surrey. It can be identified, therefore, that lack of awareness of opportunities of advanced professional education which is clinically based can be associated with the paucity of such facilities.

At district level only 24% of respondents found local post-basic educational programmes useful. Indeed, despite some very flexible attitudes in some schools of nursing, little of this seems to permeate the staff of these districts. There is clearly a need for all educational opportunity to be given greater publicity. This is really suggesting that the methods at present used, however adequate they seem, do not reach many potential recipients and that some revolutionary thinking is needed to

93

overcome this. This perhaps also applies to diploma courses. It was also noted that most programmes offered were of an *ad hoc* nature and followed no particular pattern. There was no evidence of systematic updating programmes being offered locally. In some districts there was little evidence of updating post-basic programmes of any kind. Some charge nurses stated at interview that they found it difficult to manage attendance at the few programmes available because of the vagaries of ward staffing. (This was in reference to the difficulty experienced by charge nurses in planning staff duty rosters to meet such requirements because the necessity for making up deficits of staff in other wards frequently required the redistribution of staff at short notice).

In investigating the literature relating to nursing, the researcher attempted to indicate the essential attributes of nursing and the philosophies which guide practice. The identification of the role of the charge nurse was also sought from the literature and the importance of this role in the delivery of care to patients was confirmed. Some of the stresses which exist at ward level were also demonstrated. What has not been made clear, perhaps, is the contribution of the learner nurse to the situation. A considerable proportion of the staff in any ward is untrained, many of the staff being nurses undergoing training. For the charge nurse this means that, not only do these nurses need to be trained and supervised, but also the progression of nurses through their training means that there are frequent changes of personnel and the nurse in charge is constantly managing the delivery of patient care through the services of nurses who are learning their skills and whose knowledge and abilities she/he has little time to assess and who, moreover, move on to other aspects of their training to make room for a further allocation of learner nurses. In this situation of frequent change of staff the charge nurse must ensure that the delivery of patient care is safe for patients and must also enable learner nurses to develop nursing skills both of a technical and social nature. It has been indicated in this research that little emphasis has been placed on the acquisition of interpersonal skills during training and the present overcrowded curriculum leaves little time for their development. The opportunities for teaching within the ward environment are, as Fretwell suggested, likely to be limited by the pressures to "get on with the work". There is an anomaly here, in that charge nurses, who have not been trained in teaching methods seem to be expected to "teach" in the most difficult situation of all; the stress filled and frequently work over-loaded wards of hospitals. How they teach and what they teach is never clearly defined. Pembrey (1980) suggested that nurses learn some of their skills by modelling their behaviour on that of charge nurses who exhibit such skills, and some work is at present being undertaken to enable charge nurses to acquire the skills they need by means of role based training. This experimental programme is, at present, at an early stage of development and is available only in two hospitals, and in only

94

one ward in each hospital. The existence of this one experimental training scheme for charge nurses highlights another paradox in nursing; that this role which is conceded to be a key role in the nursing care of patients has no established training to equip nurses to undertake the role. In view of this it is not surprising that opportunity to maintain knowledge or to acquire new knowledge in any systematic way is very limited.

Nurses in this study were knowledgeable about the variety of specialist training offered by the Joint Board of Clinical Nursing Studies and the necessity for such training for nurses working in specialist units was also recognised. Nurses were also well informed about training leading to registration on the supplementary registers, indicating that where opportunities for improving nursing knowledge exist, charge nurses know of them. There is also evidence from the scores on Scale 2, which records satisfaction with updating facilities, that greater proportions of charge nurses in general divisions recorded scores in the "dissatisfied" area of the scale. (45% of respondents of this grade scored 25 or below). The smaller percentage of nursing officers in this division who scored in the dissatisfied part of the scale is interesting, since there are no more opportunities for updating clinical knowledge available to nursing officers and there were no statistically significant differences in the attendance between the two groups. There were, however, statistically significant differences in the proportions of nursing officers recording local study episodes as a means of keeping up to date with nursing and a greater proportion of nursing officers found that the management training programmes met their needs. It is worth noting that nursing officers attended the same programmes available to charge nurses, suggesting that management training is geared more to the needs of nursing officers than charge nurses. This may be some support for the view expressed by Smith (1977) that the administrative aspect of the nursing officer role is the predominant aspect in the real rather than in an ideal world. However, these findings may only mean that nursing officers as a group are more satisfied generally than are charge nurses. In the case of midwives, again, a much smaller proportion recorded scores in the dissatisfied area of Scale 2. These respondents, in addition to their attendance at statutory refresher courses, recorded higher proportions attending Joint Board of Clinical Nursing Studies courses. Midwives also recorded a lower proportion of respondents who found that the management training met their needs. It may be that the very specialist nature of midwifery practice results in midwives having little interest in programmes not couched in midwifery terms; or that the greater opportunities for professional updating available to midwives make them more discriminating in their judgements.

Midwives also show statistically significant differences in the proportions who consider that refresher courses should be compulsory.

Among those who were not in favour of compulsory courses there were those whose comments showed that these midwives were considering the difficulties involved in making arrangements to live away from home for the necessary five days, not that the courses were of no value. This view was reflected by other respondents who showed a strong bias in favour of updating educational programmes being available in the home district. It was also recorded that many respondents would be prepared to contribute some of their own time to post-basic education. The usual qualification made was that such a contribution should be "reasonable".

In the responses from those who were interviewed there was little evidence that the concept of a clinical nurse consultant role was fully understood and most respondents discussed the organisational difficulties of a nurse consultant role without conceptualising the benefits which may be available to the charge nurse from this development. It is possible that such a role would evolve more easily when the development of updating and ongoing post-basic educational programmes have become a reality.

The nurses who comprised the sample in this research provided evidence that for charge nurses in the general division of nursing in this regional health authority, keeping up to date with nursing knowledge is largely a matter of individual effort unsupported by any educationally organised programmes. Not only is there evidence of little professional education orientated towards charge nurses to equip them to undertake the role, but also there is little in the way of systematic educational inputs available to such nurses after appointment. Charge nurses in this study identified a need for clinical updating and for increased knowledge of interpersonal skills (which Argyle (1967) and others posited can be taught, using a variety of methods). These have also been identified by nurses of this grade in research undertaken in other countries and suggest growing consciousness among nurses of the demands made upon those who are directly involved in the organisation of care to patients. It is manifest that despite the many opportunities available to nurses to enable them to acquire training in specialist fields (the programmes provided by the Joint Board of Clinical Nursing Studies) there is little opportunity available to charge nurses to maintain competence by means of the systematic updating of nursing knowledge and the acquisition of new knowledge and that charge nurses are aware of these deficiencies. The educational system at present available to nurses does not encompass systematic updating for trained nurses and, while it is not within the objectives of this research to consider the development of such programmes, there is evidence from respondents that there is need for considerable innovation in the provision of such education if nurses are to make use of opportunities in a way which will not only meet their own needs but will offer evidence of competence to employing authorities.

It is contended by the author that the era is passed when nurses can rely on knowledge being acquired by, as has been stated by Auld "a process of osmosis". The public has the right to expect the trained nurse, who accepts responsibility for their well-being when they become patients, to be able to meet these expectations with confidence.

The further reorganisation of the National Health Service opens up new possibilities for the structure of nursing. The literature abounds with references to a need of development of a clinical career structure for nurses and attention is drawn to the ambivalence which exists, where nurses of charge nurse grade are the most important nurse in the delivery of nursing care to patients, but the nurse lowest in the management hierarchy.

In this research charge nurses clearly stated that nursing officers are not recognised by them as experts in clinical care and they viewed nursing officers as truly managerial in that they (nursing officers) are "enablers", giving access to resources both of materials and personnel and that theirs is a role of major importance in allowing the charge nurse to concentrate on the care of patients in the ward areas. In a new structure the two clear elements of nursing responsibility could be recognised. Directors of Nursing Services, a new role envisaged, could have support from two areas:

1. Support from administrative staff recognised as being responsible for the provision of goods, services and staff to specific wards, and help from nurses with certain specialist skills in management, for example personnel skills. Educational programmes of academic credibility are needed for these nurses; progammes which could be built upon to enable those who wish to progress to more senior management posts to acquire further qualifications which would have equal status with other managers in the health service.

2. Clinical support from nurses with acknowledged clinical expertise. These nurses would be primarily available to help charge nurses and would act as consultants to ward nurses and would be responsible for increasing the body of nursing knowledge by research and for disseminating knowledge gained from local and other research programmes to nurses working with patients. A tutor could form part of a team and would offer a direct link with nursing staff who train nurse learners in addition to facilitating learning by trained nurses.

It is suggested that the structure outlined is potentially available now but that access to education to support such development is haphazard and uncoordinated, although there are already in existence programmes of training in research skills. Some of the nurses undertaking this work would be in a position to register appropriate research with universities which would lead to the award of higher degrees.

The researcher is aware that the proposed structure would result in a reduction of hierarchy since nurses outside the ward areas would be operating primarily as "enablers" in one form or another. The present pay structure for trained nurses is so wide and so varied that rationalisation to encompass this change is already both necessary and desirable.

To make such developments possible there is a need for a Learning Resource Unit at regional level to service and coordinate programmes. Educational packages containing elements of learning from social and biological sciences are needed from trained nurses which would relate more realistically to nursing needs than the present education programmes where some of the social skill learning available to charge nurses comes from management education and is, therefore, unrelated to the needs of patient care. It is also posited by the present researcher that there is a need for such educational programmes to be available locally in a form which could be built into recognisable educational units which could be linked to a reward system, as medical continuing education is linked. In such a development clinical experts, as postulated, could operate without threat to the autonomy of the charge nurse who would thus have the opportunity to maintain and expand nursing knowledge and to view career development by means of clinical expertise, in addition to teaching and management.

It is essential that nurses should not lose the opportunity, at present available to them, to produce a structure which allows, for career development and professional satisfaction.

APPENDIX A

Statistical Tests used in the Analysis of the Data

A coding frame was developed and open-ended questions were categorised by the researcher before coding. Two subsamples of questionnaires (30 in each subsample) were examined by two independent observers who checked the categorisations. Agreement was reached on these categories and the data were coded on to Cope Chat Hand Sort Cards for analysis. Because of the number of cards generated for each respondent relationships between variables could not be easily identified using this method and the data were subsequently coded for computer analysis. The Statistical Programme for the Social Sciences was used, frequencies and crosstab subprogrammes being utilised to generate descriptive data. Differences between groups were tested using chi square significance tests. The data were subsequently examined using the stepwise multiple regression subprogramme.

Chi square test of significance

The chi square statistic (X^2) can be used to test the significance of different proportions in contingency tables. It is computed by comparing two sets of frequencies, the observed frequencies and the frequencies which could be expected if no difference existed between the groups. The formula for this calculation is:

$$X^2 = \frac{\varepsilon(O-E)^2}{E}$$

When O = observed frequency
and E = expected frequency if no difference exists.
Small differences are likely to be related to chance.

The degrees of freedom influence. These are equal to:

$$(R-1)\,(C-1)$$

When R = row and C = column. The level of probability acceptable is set at $p < 0.05$.

99

The Chi square test of significance is non-parametric in nature (makes no assumptions about the nature of the distribution of the target population). It is appropriate for use with ordinal scales. When the numbers in the cells is small Yates correction is applied to the result before assuming significance. This formula is:

$$X_c^2 = \frac{(O - E - \frac{1}{2})^2}{E}$$

Another test applied to test the reality of difference in proportion encountered is the Standard Error in the difference in proportion. The formula is:

$$\sqrt{pq\left(\frac{1}{n_1} + \frac{1}{n_2}\right)}$$

when $p =$ the proportion of the sample which contains the attribute and $q =$ the proportion which does not. A difference of three times the standard error was accepted as significant.

The use of such significance testing indicates the existence of difference and estimates the probability that such difference could be due to chance alone.

Step-wise multiple regression analysis

This test enables to be determined how much of the variance in a dependent variable can be accounted for by variance in a number of independent variables. In this research the dependent variables were Scales 1 and 2 and the independent variables used were those which showed significant differences in significance tests. Stepwise multiple regression enters predictor variables sequentially into the regression equation. The variable with the greatest influence is entered first and subsequent variables entered show the amount of influence exerted by the remaining variables on the dependent variable, when the effects of the preceding variables have been removed.

More detailed information on statistical tests is available in the texts devoted to the topic. The following have been useful to the writer:

BAHN, A. K. (1972) Basic Medical Statistics. New York, Grune and Stratton Ltd.
BLALOCK, H. M. (1960) Social Statistics. New York, McGraw-Hill.
MORONEY, M. J. (1970) Facts from Figures. London, Penguin.
TYRRELL, M. (1975) Using Numbers for Effecting Health Service Management. London, Heinemann.

APPENDIX B

Characteristics of the Sample

Certain characteristics have been established as being influential in shaping respondents' views on professional updating (Berg, 1973; Cooper, 1966). These variables are described in the following Tables:

Frequency Tables

TABLE A.

Frequencies by Grade, Specialty and Hospital Size

General nurses numbered	241	(85%)
Midwives.......................................	43	(15%)
	284	
Nursing officers numbered......................	35	(12%)
Charge nurses..................................	249	(88%)
	284	
Staff from 'large' hospitals	136	(48%)
Staff from 'small' hospitals	148	(52%)
	284	

The above relate to the patterns produced by stratification of the sample.

Random selection produced the following:

TABLE B
Frequency by Sex

Males numbered.................................	42	(15%)
Females..	242	(85%)
	284	

This 15% of the sample who are male nurses is close to the national proportion of male registered nurses of 16% (CNO. Report, Nursing

101

1974–1976). The proportion of senior staff is interesting; 21% of nursing officers are males. This distribution of males among senior nurses has also been noted by Jones (1979). Austen (1977) suggested that the present managerial structure in nursing encourages advancement among males more than females, since, she states, "...masculine knowledge input is widely regarded as valuable, not least by the leaders of the profession."

Re-examining the category "general nurses" into "Type of nursing" we find that:

TABLE C
Frequency by Type of Nursing

Medical/Surgical number	117	(41%)
Geriatric area number	47	(16%)
Specialty area number*	77	(27%)
Midwifery area number**	43	(15%)
	284	

*Includes areas such as operating theatres, outpatient departments, intensive therapy units, ophthalmic units, radiotherapy.
**All staff recorded as working in maternity areas are trained practising midwives.

Length of time qualified showed the following distribution:

TABLE D
Frequency by Length of Time qualified

Less than 5 years	35	(12%)
5 but less than 15 years	92	(32%)
15 but less than 25 years	87	(31%)
25 or more years	70	(25%)
	284	

71% of those qualified less than 5 years were married. 61% of all others were married.

TABLE E
Frequency by Small Hospitals

100 but less than 200	64	(22% of sample)
50 but less than 199	28	(10% of sample)
less than 50 beds 100	56	(20% of sample)
	148	

102

Table F
Frequency by Marital Status

Married	151	(53%)
Unmarried	102	(36%)
Other (widowed, separated or divorced)	31	(11%)
	284	

Since responses from the "other" category did not differ from the married group the two groups were amalgamated for the purposes of analysis.

Shift patterns showed:

Table G
Frequency by Shift Patterns

Night duty staff numbered	59	(21%)
Day duty staff numbered	225	(79%)
	284	

Table H
Dependents and Marital Status

Those who recorded dependents were:

Married	100	(55%)
Unmarried	27	(26%)
	127	

Letter of Introduction

Dear

How Can Trained Nurses 'Keep Up'?

This questionnaire is part of a survey intended to discover if trained nurses, those of charge nurses and nursing officer grades, feel a need to update their knowledge and what facilities they consider they need to enable them to do this.

I know how busy you are (I myself work full time as a nurse) but feel justified in asking for your help since there is little information available on the subject and qualified nurses themselves are most likely to be aware if a need exists.

The information on the introductory page is very important since it will allow me to assess any local or special circumstances which may influence individual views. All information obtained will be confidential and individuals will not be identified. A code number will enable me to send a reminder to anyone who has forgotten to return the questionnaire.

The research takes place in the—Region and is registered with the University of Surrey.

I am very grateful for your help in this matter and enclose a stamped addressed envelope for the questionnaire which I hope you will return before.......

Yours sincerely,
(Mrs. Mary Stapleton)

Questionnaire

"Ongoing Educational Needs of Trained Nurses"

Please tick relevant box.

Grade: [6][7] Part time ☐ Night duty ☐ Male ☐ Unmarried ☐ Widowed ⎫
                                                   Divorced ⎬ ☐
        Full time ☐ Day duty ☐ Female ☐ Married ☐ Separated ⎭

Home Commitments
Responsible for someone 16 years and under.   Yes ☐   No ☐
Responsible for someone over 16 years. Yes ☐   No ☐

Nurse training:
Did you train in this country?   Yes ☐   No ☐
If 'No', please state which country ....
Are you a state certified midwife?   Yes ☐   No ☐
Do you practise as a midwife?   Yes ☐   No ☐

Length of time qualified:

Less than 5 years. ☐
5 years but less than 15 years ☐
15 years but less than 25 years ☐
25 or more years ☐

Type of Nursing

Geriatric ☐	OR Specialty:	I.T.U. ☐	Theatre ☐	E.N.T. ☐
Medical ☐		C.C.U. ☐	A & E ☐	Ophthalmic ☐
Surgical ☐		Renal ☐		Orthopaedic ☐
				Neurological ☐

Other ....

Please tick relevant box.

Size of Hospital:

Less than 50 beds
50 beds or more but less than 100 beds
100 beds or more but less than 200 beds
200 or more beds

Travelling

Is your travelling time   (a)   Less than $\frac{1}{2}$ hour?
to work: (b) $\frac{1}{2}$ hour or more but less than 1 hour?
                                (c)   1 hour or more but less than 2 hours
                                (d)   2 or more hours?

This section of the questionnaire relates to the opportunities available to you to use books and journals as a means of keeping up to date with nursing.

1. (a)   Which journals are available, in your hospital, for you to to read?
    A. *Nursing Times*
    B. *Queen's Nursing Journal*
    C. *Midwives Chronicle*
    D. *Health & Social Service Journal*
    E. *American Journal of Nursing*
    F. *Nursing Weekly*
    G. *Nursing Mirror*
    H. *British Medical Journal*
    I. *New Society*
    J. *The Lancet*
    K. *Nursing Chronicle*
    L. *New Scientist*
    M. *Journal of Obstetrics & Gynaecology
        of the British Commonwealth*
    N. *Pharmaceutical Journal*
    O. *Midwife, H. V. & Community Nurse*
    P. Any others. . . . .
    . . . .

   (b)   Are there journals conveniently placed for you to browse through?

                    Yes ☐   No ☐

         If 'Yes',
   (c)   Where are they available? (Please identify the journal, using the appropriate letter).

                Journal   *Place*
         . . . .
         . . . .
         . . . .

106

Please tick relevant box.

2. (a)   Do professional journals circulate through your working area?

Yes ☐ No ☐

If 'Yes',
   (b)   Could you identify these, using the appropriate letter?

   ....
   ....

3. (a)   Do you have the opportunity to read a nursing
           journal?   Yes ☐ No ☐
   (b)   Have you read one:
           (i) this week?   ☐
           (ii) this month?   ☐
           (iii) in the last 3 months?   ☐

Did you:

           (i) buy these?   ☐
           (ii) have them supplied?   ☐
           (iii) get them from any other source?   ☐

   ....

4. (a)   Do you have the opportunity to read a medical
                                    journal?   Yes ☐ No ☐
   (b)   have you read one:

           (i) this week?   ☐
           (ii) this month?   ☐
           (iii) in the last 3 months?   ☐
   ....

5.   Do you think there is any need for trained nurses to read:

           (a) nursing journals?   Yes ☐ No ☐
           (b) medical journals   Yes ☐ No ☐

   ....
   ....

Different types of library facilities are available for nurses. From the
statements below could you identify the kind of libraries which are available to
you for reference and loan purposes?

6. (a)   Library for learners only.   ☐
   (b)   Library for learners which trained nurses may use for   ☐
           reference purposes.
   (c)   Library designed to meet the needs of trained nurses.   ☐

107

Please tick relevant box.

6.   Continued...

   (d)   Library whose facilities are designed to meet the
         needs of all nurses. ☐

   (e)   Library designed to be used by all trained staff. ☐

7.   (a)   Do the libraries available in your district contain books and
           journals which you consider useful?   Yes ☐ No ☐

   . . . .

   (b)   Do the facilities meet:
         (i) all your needs? ☐
         (ii) some of your needs? ☐
         (iii) none of your needs? ☐

8.   (a)   Have you used a professional library in your district:

         (i) in the last week? ☐
         (ii) in the last month? ☐
         (iii) in the last year? ☐

   (b)   Have you used any other library for professional purposes,
         during the last year?   Yes ☐ No ☐

   . . . .
   . . . .
   . . . .

9.   I have drawn a thermometer which ranges from 'very satisfied'
     to 'very dissatisfied'.

     very satisfied

     very dissatisfied

     Could you mark on this, with a line, how satisfied you feel with
     the journal/library facilities which are available to you, to
     enable you to keep up-to-date with nursing?

108

Please tick relevant box.

The next section of the questionnaire is concerned with other ways in which you keep up-to-date with nursing knowledge.

10. (a) Do consultants' rounds help you keep your professional knowledge up-to-date? Yes ☐ No ☐

....
....

(b) Apart from consultants rounds, what facilities are available to keep your professional knowledge up-to-date?

....
....

11. (a) Do you know of any post-basic course for nurses which you could attend?
Please list ....
any that ....
you can. ....
remember ....
....

(b) Have you attended any of these courses?
(Include *any* training you have had since state registration).

Course	Year
....	....
....	....
....	....
....	....

(c) Did these courses meet your needs? Yes ☐ No ☐

....
....

12. Is there a nurse specifically in charge of education for qualified nurses in your district? Yes ☐ No ☐

13. (a) Are there ongoing educational programmes planned for trained nurses? (Sisters study days might be used for this). Yes ☐ No ☐

Can you list those available in the last 12 months:
....
....

(b) Are there study periods based on one main topic around which a series of lectures/seminars are arranged? Yes ☐ No ☐

Approximately how many topics in the last 12 months?
....

Please tick relevant box.

14.   Are there any programmes available to you to enable you to develop the teaching skills required of you in your ward or department?   Yes ☐ No ☐

. . . .

15.   Could you list any subjects which you consider could usefully be studied by nurses in charge of wards and departments to help them develop and maintain the skills required of them?

. . . .
. . . .

16.   Have you attended a management training course?
      Yes ☐ No ☐

      If 'Yes',
17. (a) Did the course meet your needs?   Yes ☐ No ☐

    (b) Did it relate to your work?   Yes ☐ No ☐

        Any comments. . . . .
        . . . .

    (c) Where there aspects of management theory about which you wished to know more?   Yes ☐ No ☐

    (d) Were there aspects of management practice about which you wished to know more?   Yes ☐ No ☐

18.   I have drawn a thermometer again so that you can indicate, with a line, how satisfied you feel with the training/educational facilities available to you to enable you to keep up-to-date with nursing.

very satisfied

very dissatisfied

Please tick relevant box.

The next section is concerned with your views on the way to meet any needs that trained nurses may have for updating nursing knowledge.

19. (a)   Do you feel any need to update your nursing knowledge?

Great Need	Some Need	Little Need	No Need

(b)   Do you have the opportunity to update nursing knowledge?

Too much	Adequate	Some	No opportunity

Different types of educational programmes are available for adults. Please tick the type you prefer.

20. (a)   Some one to talk to you—the lecture type of programme.
Yes ☐ No ☐

(b)   The opportunity to talk around a subject—the group discussion/seminar type of programme.   Yes ☐ No ☐

(c)   You may like both of these or neither, if there is some other approach which seems to you to be appropriate, could you list some details of this?
....
....
....

21. (i)   Which of the following study arrangements would you be able to attend?
(Please tick all of those you would find possible)

(a) Full time, away from your own district?
(b) Part time, away from your own district?
(c) Full time, in your own district?
(d) Part time, in your own district?
(e) A course you could attend in your own time?

....
....

(ii)   Is the time span of such courses important to you? (Please tick whichever one of the following applies to you).

(a) One day at a time only.
(b) One week (Mon—Fri) at a time only.
(c) One month at a time only.
(d) Longer than any of these. (Please state limits)

....

111

Please tick relevant box.

21. Continued...

    (iii)   Are the number of hours you are away from home per day a consideration? (From the following statements, please tick the one which applies to you).

        (a)   Hours must come within normal working and travelling time.

        (b)   Hours could be extended (Please state limits). ⊟

        ....

        (c)   Time would not be a problem. ☐

        (d)   Any further comments ....
        ....

22. (a)   Do you consider it useful to have short courses of study available to trained nurses as an on-going programme from which they could choose?   Yes ☐ No ☐

        ....

        If 'Yes',
  (b)   Should attendance be voluntary?   Yes ☐ No ☐

  (c)   Should attendance be compulsory?   Yes ☐ No ☐

        ....

  (d)   Do you consider it useful to have refresher courses every few years? (Midwives already have these).   Yes ☐ No ☐

        If 'Yes',

  (e)   Should attendance be voluntary?   Yes ☐ No ☐

  (f)   Should attendance be compulsory?   Yes ☐ No ☐

        ....
        ....

23.   Have you found that basic training in nursing has been enough to enable you to undertake the work required of you in your ward or department?   Yes ☐ No ☐

        ....
        ....

Thank you very much for completing this questionnaire.

Are there any comments you would like to make on this subject, either to expand an area which I have touched on or to introduce an aspect which I have missed? I shall be very grateful for any information you care to offer.

Interview Check List

1. Questionnaire, sections 1, 2 and 3
2. Recent changes: Re-organisation
   Salmon structure
   Have they affected you in your work?
3. What about career prospects—are they better?
   worse?
   no different?
4. Would efforts to keep up to date with nursing affect the time spent with patients?

   Would any time spent have an effect on patient care?
5. Is updating or nursing knowledge:
   (a)   encouraged?
   (b)   taken for granted?
   (c)   treated with indifference?
   (d)   discouraged?
6. Does systematic updating take place now?
   (explain systematic)
7. Define Clinical Nurse Consultant:
   Is it known?
   Is it a possible development?
   Would you consider it?

References

ABEL-SMITH, B. (1977) *A History of the Nursing Profession*. London, Heinemann.

ABDELLAH, F. G. and LEVINE, E. (1965) *Better Patient Care through Nursing Research*. New York, MacMillan.

ANDERSON, E. R. (1973) *The Role of the Nurse*. London, Royal College of Nursing.

ARGYLE, M. (1967) *The Psychology of Interpersonal Behaviour*. London, Penguin.

ARGYRIS, C. (1957) *Personality—Organisation*. Harper International. Student Reprint.

AULD, M. (1979) Nursing in a Changing Society. *Journal of Advanced Nursing*, **4**, 287–298.

AUSTEN, R. (1976) *Occupation and Profession in the Organisation of Nursing Work*. Ph.D. Thesis, University of Wales.

AUSTEN, R. (1977) Sex and Gender in the Future of Nursing. *Nursing Times*, **73**, (34–35) Occasional Papers, 113–119.

AUSTEN, R. (1978) Professionalisation and the Nature of Nursing Reward. *Journal of Advanced Nursing*, **3**, (1) 9–123.

BAGLEY, C. (1974) Nursing the Salmon Way. *Health and Social Service Journal*, **84**, (4374) 359–360.

BAGLEY, C. (1977) *Anomie and Alienation*. Paper to VIII World Congress of Sociology, Toronto, August, 1977.

BALY, M. (1973) *Nursing and Social Change*. London, Heinemann Medical Books Ltd.

BANTON, M. (1965) *Roles*. London, Tavistock Publications.

BENDALL, E. R. D. and RAYBOULD, E. (1969) *A History of the General Nursing Council for England and Wales, 1919–1969*. London, Lewis.

BENDALL, E. (1973) Nursing Attitudes in the Health Care Team. *Nursing Times*, **69**, (7) Occasional Papers, 25–27.

BENDALL, E. (1975) The Mistakes of 50 years, Cited by A. Dunn, *Nursing Times* **71**, (39) 1526–1527.

BENNEY, M., REISMAN, D. and STARR, S. (1956) Age and Sex in the Interview. *American Journal of Sociology*, **62**, (2) 143–152.

BENNEY, M. and HUGHES, E. C. (1956) Of Sociology and the Interview. *American Journal of Sociology*, **62**, (2) 137–141.

BERG, H. (1973) *Participant and Non-participant Nurses in Continuing Education*. D. Ed., Thesis, Columbia University.

BERGMAN, R. (1979) *Role Selection and Preparation of Unit Head Nurses*. Report to Tel Aviv University of Sackler School of Medicine, School of Continuing Medical Education, Department of Nursing.

BILODEAU, C. (1969) *Acquisition of Skill*. London, Academic Press.

BLAU, P. M. and SCOTT, R. C. (1963) *Formal Organisations*. London, Routledge and Kegan Paul.

BROWN, A. F. (1958) *Research in Nursing*. Philadelphia, W. B. Saunders Co.

114

BURGESS, G. R. (1978) Self-assessment of Continuing Education Needs. *International Nursing Review*, **25**, (3) 89–92.

BURNS, T. and STALKER, G. M. (1961) *The Management of Innovation*. London, Tavistock Publications Ltd.

BURNS, M. (1972) *An Analysis of the American Journal of Nursing as a Resource for the Self Education of Nurses*. D.Ed. Thesis, Boston University. (Unpublished).

BURTT-JONES (1980) Letter to *Nursing Times*, **76**, (43) 1879.

CARMEL, M. J. (1975) What Standards for Standards? *Library Association Rec*. **77**, (10).

CARR, A. (1978) Work of the Nursing Officer. *Nursing Times*, **74**, (34) Occasional Papers, 1417–1420.

CARR-SAUNDERS, A. M. and WILSON, P. A. (1933) *The Professions*. Oxford, Clarendon Press.

CATNACK, A. and HOUGHTON, M. (1961) *Report on Pilot Investigation of Teaching in Nurse Training Schools*. (Unpublished) S.W. Metropolitan Area Nurse Training Committee.

CARTWRIGHT, A. (1964) *Human Relations and Hospital Care*. London, Routledge and Kegan Paul.

CARTWRIGHT, F. F. (1977) *A Social History of Medicine*. London, Longman.

CASTLEDINE, G. (1977) Report on Annual Conference of Rcn Association of Nursing Practice. *Nursing Mirror*, **145**, (13) 3.

CHAPMAN, C. (1974) Nursing Education Curriculum Content. *Queens Nursing Journal*, **17**, (7) 149–152.

CHAPMAN, C. (1976) *Towards a Theory of Nursing Care*. M.Phil. Thesis, University of London.

CHAPMAN, C. (1977) *Sociology for Nurses*. (Nurses Aids Series) London, Baillière Tindall.

CHAPMAN, C. (1977) *Image of the Nurse*. Paper presented at International Council of Nurses, 16th Quadrennial Congress, Tokyo, Japan (June 3).

CLARKE, M. (1978) Planning Nursing Care. *Nursing Times*, **74**, (5) Occasional Papers, 17–20.

COLLIERE, M. F. (1980) Nursing: Thoughts on Nursing Service and Identification of the Service Offered. *International Nursing Review*, **27**, (2) 49–50.

CONLEY, A. (1972) *Instructional Leadership in Curriculum Development in Baccalaureate Programmes*. D.Ed. Thesis, Columbia University. (Unpublished).

COOPER, S. (1966) *The Continuing Learner in Nursing*. University Extension Division, Department of Nursing, University of Wisconsin.

COOPER, S. (1970) Continuing Education for Nurses. *Wisconsin Medical Journal*, **69**, 21–23.

CORNEL, M. and COLES, R. (1979) *Planning the Care of the Elderly:* Report West Sussex Area Health Authority. (Unpublished).

CORWIN, R. (1961) Role Conception and Career Aspiration. *The Sociological Quarterly*. (April), 69–86.

DARMASTAATER, J. (1977) Mandatory Continuing Education for Re-Licensing. *Journal of Nursing Care*, **10**, (3) 26.

DAVIES, C. (1976) Experience of Dependency and Control in Work: the Case of Nurses. *Journal of Advanced Nursing*, **1**, (4) 273–282.

DAVIES, C. (1971) *An Evaluation of First Line Management Training Courses for Ward Sisters in the Manchester Region.* The Centre for Business Research.

DAVIES, C. (1977) Continuities in the Development of Hospital Nursing in Britain. *Journal of Advanced Nursing,* **2,** (5) 479–493.

DAVIES, C. (1980) Past and Present in Nursing Education. *Nursing Times,* **76,** (39) 1703–1707.

DEPARTMENT OF HEALTH AND SOCIAL SECURITY, SCOTTISH HOME AND HEALTH DEPARTMENT, AND WELSH OFFICE (1972) *Report of the Committee on Nursing* (Chairman: A. Briggs), London, HMSO.

DEPARTMENT OF HEALTH AND SOCIAL SECURITY (1979) *Royal Commission on the National Health Service.* London, HMSO.

DEVINE, B. (1978) Nurse Physician Interaction Status and Social Structure within Two Hospital Wards. *Journal of Advanced Nursing,* **3,** (3) 287–295.

DEWAR, H. A. (1966) Letter. *The Lancet,* 11, (7472) 1074.

DEWAR, H. A. (1978) The Hospital Nurse after Salmon and Briggs. *Journal of the Royal Society of Medicine,* **71,** (6) 399–405.

DINGWALL, R. and MCINTOSH, J. (1978) *Readings in the Sociology of Nursing.* Introduction, 1. Edinburgh, Churchill Livingstone.

DIXON, W. and MASSEY, F. J. (1969) *Introduction to Statistical Analysis.* New York, McGraw-Hill Book Company.

DODD, A. (1973) *Towards an Understanding of Nursing.* Ph.D. Thesis, University of London. (Unpublished).

DONNISON, J. (1977) *Midwives and Medical Men.* London, Heinemann.

DRUCKER, P. F. (1965) *Educational Revolution.* Education, Economy and Society 15. Halsey A. H., Floud, J. and Arnold Anderson, C. (ed.) New York, The Free Press.

ETZIONI, A. (1969) *The Semi-professions–Nursing, Teaching and Social Work.* New York, The Free Press.

EXCHAQUET, N. (1967) The Role of the Head Nurse in the Management of the Ward. *International Nursing Review,* **14,** (5) 10–12.

FELGATE, R. V. R. (1977) *The Emergence of Militancy in the Nursing Profession 1960–1972.* Ph.D. Thesis, University of Surrey. (Unpublished).

FERGUSON, M. C. (1976) Nursing at the Crossroads. *Journal of Advanced Nursing,* **1,** (3) 237–242.

FISHER, R. F. and STRANK, R. A. (1971) Investigation into Reading Habits of Qualified Nurses. *Nursing Times,* **67,** (8) 245–247.

FOUCAULT, M. (1973) *The Birth of the Clinic* (Translated from French—A. A. Sheridan Smith). London, Tavistock Publications.

FRETWELL, J. (1980) *Enquiry into the Ward Learning Environment.* Ph.D. Thesis, University of Warwick. (Unpublished).

GALTUNG, J. (1967) *Theory and Methods of Social Research.* London, George Allen and Unwin.

GENERAL NURSING COUNCIL (1980) Library Services. Circulated April, 1980.

GEORGOPOULAS, B. S. and MANN, F. C. (1972) The Hospital as an Organisation. In: Gartly, J. E. (ed.) *Patients, Physicians and Illness,* New York, The Free Press.

GILBERT, B. B. (1966) *The Evolution of National Insurance in Great Britain.* London, Michael Joseph Ltd.

GILBERTSON, D. W. (1977) with Butterfield S. and Gill I. The Ward Sister: a Suitable Case for Treatment. *International Nursing Review,* **24,** (4) 108–113.

116

GILLESPIE (1978) Letter to *Nursing Times*, **74**, (41) 1688.

GODDARD, H. A. (1953) *The Work of Nurses in Hospital Wards*. London, Nuffield Provincial Hospitals Trust.

GODDARD, H. A. (1963) *Work Measurement as a Basis for Calculating Establishment*. Leeds, Leeds Regional Hospital Board.

GOFFMAN, E. (1961) *Asylums*. London, Pelican.

GOLDIAC, K. (1977) *Continuing Education a "Must" for Maintaining Competence*. Paper presented at International Council of Nurses, 16th Quadrennial Congress, Tokyo, Japan (May 30).

GRAHAM, J. A. G. (1980) On the State of the Profession. *Nursing Times*, **76**, (5) 186–187.

GREBNIK, E. (1970) Statistical Surveys. In: FORCESE, D. and RICHER, S. (eds.) *Stages of Social Research*. New Jersey, Prentice-Hall Inc.

GREEN, M. (1978) *The Examination of the Professionalism of Nursing in Great Britain and its Concomitant Status Implications*. M. Ed. Thesis, University of London. (Unpublished).

GROSS, MASON and MCEACHERN (1958) *Explorations in Role Analysis*. New York, John Wiley & Sons Inc.

GROSVENOR P. (1978) Nursing in Theory 1972/77. *Nursing Times*, **177**, (22) Occasional Papers, 85–87.

HAGBURG, (1970) *Stages of Social Research*. FORCESE, P. and RICHER, S. (eds.) New Jersey, Prentice-Hall Inc.

HALL, C. (1973) Who Controls the Nursing Profession. *Nursing Times*, **69**, (23) Occasional Papers, 89–91.

HECTOR, W. (1973) *Mrs. Bedford Fenwick and the Rise of Professional Nursing*. London, Royal College of Nursing.

HENDERSON, V. (1978) The Concept of Nursing. *Journal of Advanced Nursing*, **3**, (2) 113–130.

HENDERSON, V. (1968) *Basic Principles of Nursing Care*. International Council of Nurses. Karger, Basle.

HENDERSON, V. (1980) Preserving the Essence of Nursing in a Technological Age. *Journal of Advanced Nursing*, **5**, (3) 245–260.

HUNTER, T. D. (1971) New Ways in Health Care Management. *British Hospital Journal and Social Service Review*, **81**, (4237) 1319–1320.

ILLICH, J. (1976) *Limits to Medicine*. London, Marion Boyars.

JOHNSON, M. M. and MARTIN, H. W. (1958) A Sociological Analysis of the Nurse Role. *The American Journal of Nursing*, **58**, (3) 373–377.

JOHNSON, M. (1978) Nursing Auxiliaries and Nurse Professionalisation. *Nursing Times*, **74**, (8) 313–317.

JONES, D. (1979) The Role of the Nursing Officer. Paper to Royal College of Nursing Research Society. (October 3).

KATZ, F. E. (1969) *Nurses in the Semi-professions and their Organisations*. Etzioni, A. (ed.) 54–76. New York, The Free Press.

KELLY, K. (1966) Clinical Inference in Nursing. *Nursing Research*, **15**, (1) 23–26.

KENNEDY, R. (1980) Unmasking Medicine. *The Listener*, (November 13) 641–643.

KERRANE, T. (1977) American Nursing. *Health and Social Service Journal*, **37**, (4556) 1244.

KRAUSZ, E. and MILLER, S. (1974) *Social Research Design*. London, Longman Group Ltd.

LAMOND, N. (1974) *Becoming a Nurse*. London, Royal College of Nursing.

LANCET (1932) Report of the Lancet Commission on Nursing.

LELEAN, S. (1973) *Ready for Report Nurse?* London, Royal College of Nursing.

LELEAN, S. (1977) *Communications of Instructions for Nursing Care in Medical Wards*. Ph.D. Thesis, University of Surrey. (Unpublished).

LINDZEY, G. and ARONSON, E. (1954) *Handbook of Social Psychology*. London, Addison-Wesley.

LUCK, G. M., LUCKMAN, J., SMITH, B. W. and STRINGER, J. (1971) *Patients, Hospitals and Operational Research*. London, Tavistock Publications.

LYSAUGHT, J. P. (1970) Continuing Education Necessity and Opportunity. *Journal of Continuing Education in Nursing*, **1**, (3) 5–10.

MANN, P. H. (1971) *Methods of Sociological Enquiry*. Oxford, Blackwells Sociology Series.

MACGUIRE, J. M. (1964) *Recruitment and Wastage from Adult Training Programmes with Particular Reference to Nursing*. Ph.D. Thesis, University of London. (Unpublished).

MACKENZIE, W. J. M. (1979) *Power and Responsibility in Health Care*. Published for Nuffield Provincial Hospitals Trust, London, Oxford University Press.

MACLEAN, U. (1974) *Nursing in Contemporary Society*. London, Routledge and Kegan Paul.

MCFARLANE, J. (1976) A Charter for Caring. *The Journal of Advanced Nursing*, **1**, (3) 196–197.

MCGHEE, A. (1961) *The Patient's Attitude to Nursing Care*. Edinburgh, E. and S. Livingstone Ltd.

MARSON, S. N. (1979) *Creating a Climate for Learning*. National Health Service Learning Resources Unit, Sheffield Polytechnic.

MELIA, K. M. (1979) A Sociological Approach to the Analysis of Nursing Work. *Journal of Advanced Nursing*, **4**, (1) 57–67.

MENZIES, I. (1960) *A Case Study in the Functioning of Social Systems as a Defence against Anxiety*. London, Tavistock Publications.

MERTON, R. K. (1957) *Social Theory and Social Structure*. Illinois, The Free Press.

MERTON, R. K. (1960) The Search for Professional Status. *The American Journal of Nursing*, **60**, (5) 662–663.

MINISTRY OF HEALTH AND BOARD OF EDUCATION (1939) *Interdepartmental Committee on Nursing Services: Interim Report*. (Chairman: Earl of Athlone) London, HMSO.

MINISTRY OF HEALTH, DEPARTMENT OF HEALTH FOR SCOTLAND, MINISTRY OF LABOUR AND NATIONAL SERVICE (1947). *The Recruitment and Training of Nurses*. (Chairman: R. Wood) London, HMSO.

MINISTRY OF HEALTH, SCOTTISH HOME AND HEALTH DEPARTMENT (1966) *Report of the Committee on Senior Nursing Staff Structure*. (Chairman: B. Salmon) London, HMSO.

MOSER, C. A. and KALTON, G. (1972) *Survey Methods in Social Investigation*. London, Heinemann Educational Books Ltd.

NIGHTINGALE, F. (1970) *Notes on Nursing*. London, G. Duckworth.

NURSING TIMES (1977) Continuing Education. Council of National Representatives Meeting, International Council of Nurses. Leader, *Nursing Times*, **73**, (25) 933.

118

O'CONNOR, A. (1979) Reasons Nurses Participate in Continuing Education. *Nursing Research*, **28**, (6) 354–359.

OGIER, M. (1979) *The Effect of Ward Sisters' Management Style upon Nurse Learners*. Paper presented at the Royal College of Nursing Research Society Annual Conference, Nottingham University.

ONGLEY, V. M. (1976) Nursing Officer Clinical Specialist or Administrator. *Nursing Mirror*, **142**, (6) 57–61.

OPPENHEIM, A. N. (1966) *Questionnaire Design and Attitude Measurement*. London, Heinemann Books on Sociology.

ORR, J. (1979) Nursing and the Process of Scientific Enquiry. *Journal of Advanced Nursing*, **4**, (6) 603–610.

PARSONS, T. (1972) Definitions of Health and Illness in the Light of American Values and Structures. In: JACO, E. G. (ed.) *Patients, Physicians and Illness*. New York, The Free Press.

PARSONS, T. (1957) *The Social System*. New York, The Free Press.

PEMBREY, S. (1978) *The Role of the Ward Sister in the Management of Nursing*. Ph.D. Thesis, University of Edinburgh. (Unpublished).

PEMBREY, S. (1980) *The Ward Sister—Key to Nursing*. London, Royal College of Nursing.

PEPPER, R. (1977) *Professionalism, Training and Work. Study of Nursing in a General Hospital*. Ph.D. Thesis, University of Kent. (Unpublished).

PINKER, R. (1978) A Nurse for All Seasons. *Nursing Mirror*, **146**, (21) 31–34.

QUENZER, R. (1974) *The Development of Patient Centred Behaviour Patterns in Nurse Training*. M.Ed. Thesis, University of Manchester. (Unpublished).

REVANS, R. W. (1962) Hospital Attitudes and Communications. *The Sociological Review*, (Monograph No. 5 July). University of Keele.

REVANS, R. W. (1964) *Standards for Morale: Cause and Effect in Hospitals*. Nuffield Provincial Hospitals Trust, London. Oxford University Press.

ROEM, M. (1974) The Continuing Education Unit—a New Concept of Measurement. *Journal of Nursing Administration*, **4**, (2) 56–59.

ROGERS, A. (1978) Today's Nurses. *Nursing Mirror*, **146**, (2) 7.

ROPER, N. (1976) *Clinical Experience in Nurse Education*, (Department of Nursing Studies, Monograph No. 5) University of Edinburgh.

ROSEN, C. and ROSEN, H. (1973) *The Language of Primary School Children*. London, Penguin.

ROWBOTTOM, R. (1971) Emerging Patterns of Hospital Organisation. *Health and Social Service Journal*, **81**, (4229) 872–875.

ROWLAND, M. (1976) *The Role of the Nursing Officer in the Croydon Area: Report*. Croydon Area Health Authority. (Unpublished).

ROYAL COMMISSION ON MEDICAL EDUCATION. *Report of the Royal Commission on Medical Education 1965–68*. (Chairman: The Rt. Hon. the Lord Todd) London, HMSO.

RUDD, T. D. (1973) Anxiety in Nursing. *Health and Social Service Journal*, **83**, (4366) 2999–3000.

ROYAL COLLEGE OF NURSING (1964) *A Reform of Nursing Education: Report of a Special Committee on Nurse Education*. (Chairman: Sir Harry Platt) London, Royal College of Nursing.

ROYAL COLLEGE OF NURSING (1943) *Nursing Reconstruction Committee Report*. (Chairman: Lord Horder) London, Royal College of Nursing.

119

SAUNDERS, L. (1954) The Changing Role of Nurses. *American Journal of Nursing*, **54**, (9) 1094–1098.

SCHLOTFELDT, R. (1965) The Nurses' View of the Changing Nurse—Physician Relationship. *Journal of Medical Education*, **40** (8) 772–777.

SCHURR, M. (1968) *Leadership and the Nurse*. London, English Universities Press Ltd.

SCHULMAN, S. (1972) Mother Surrogate after a Decade. In: JACO, E. G. (ed.) *Patients, Physicians and Illness*. New York, Free Press.

SCOTTISH NATIONAL NURSING and MIDWIFERY CONSULTATIVE COMMITTEE (1976) *A New Concept in Nursing*. Edinburgh. The Scottish Home and Health Department.

SCOTT-WRIGHT, M. (1971) Progress and Prospects in Nursing Research. *Nursing Times*, **67**, (3) Occasional Papers, 9–12.

SENIOR, O. E. (1978) Nurse/Patient Dependency. *Management Services*, (October), 4–8.

SEYMER, L. R. (1956) *A General History of Nursing*. London, Faber and Faber.

SMART, G. A. (1974) Keeping up a Concern on Both Sides of the Atlantic. *Hospital Practice* (July), 160.

SMART, P. (1972) *Thinking and Reasoning*. London, MacMillan Education Ltd.

SMITH, J. (1976) *Sociology and Nursing*. Edinburgh, Livingstone Nursing Texts.

SMITH, J. (1977) Nursing Officers. *Journal of Advanced Nursing* **2**, (6) 571–588.

SOUTH, J. F. (1857) *Factors Relating to Hospital Nurses*. (Pamphlet) London.

SOUTHALL, A. (1959) An Operational Theory of Role. *Human Relations* **12**, (1) 17.

STACEY, M. (1969) *Methods of Social Research*. Oxford, Pergamon Press.

STAUNTON, M. (1979) New Dimensions of Professional Responsibility. *International Nursing Review*, **26**, (3) 84–85.

STEWART, R. (1970) *The Reality of Organisations*. London, MacMillan and Co. Ltd.

STUDDY, S. (1980) Continuing Education: American Attitudes. *Nursing Focus*, **2**, (1) 9–10.

SUSSMAN, M. B. (1971) Reflections on the Organisation of Social Research. In: O'TOOLE, R. (ed.) *Organisation, Management and Tactics of Social Research*. Cambridge, Schenkman Publishing Co. Ltd.

TABOR, R. B. (1979) Professional Knowledge and the Nurse. *Nursing Times*, **75**, (46), 1983–4.

TAGLIACOZZO, D. L. and MAUKSCH, H. O. (1972) The Patients' View of the Patients' Role. In: JACO, E. G. (ed.) *The Patients, Physicians and Illness*. New York, The Free Press.

TARITSANO, B. J. (1971) *Perceptions of Hospital Personnel Regarding Continuing Education for Hospital Staff Nurses*. Ph.D. Thesis, University of Nebraska. (Unpublished).

WALKER, V. H. (1967) *Nursing and Ritualistic Practice*. New York, MacMillan and Co.

WALL, T. and HESPE, G. (1972) The Attitudes of Nurses Towards the Salmon Structure. *Nursing Times*, **68**, (27) Occasional Papers, 105–108.

WEBB, E. S. (1947) Unconventionality, Triangulation and Inference. In:

DENZIN, N. K. (ed.) *Sociological Methods*. New York, McGraw Hill

WEBER, M. (1974) *The Theory of Social and Economic Organisations*. (Translated by HENDERSON, A. M. and PARSONS. T.) New York, The Free Press.

WHITE, R. (1975) *The Development of the Poor Law Nursing Service and the Political Medical and Social Factors that Influenced it 1845–1948*. M.Sc. Thesis, University of Manchester. (Unpublished).

WHITEHEAD, A. (1932) *The Aims of Education* (Technical Education and Its Relationship to Science and Literature). London, Williams and Norgate.

WILENSKY, H. L. (1964) Professionalism of Everyone. *American Journal of Sociology* **70**, (2) 137.

WILLIAMS, D. (1969) The Administrative Contribution of the Nursing Sister. *Public Administration,* **47**, (3) 307–325.

WILLIAMS, J. A. (1970) Interviewer Role Performance. A further Note on Bias in Information Interview. In: FORCESE, D. P. and RICHER, S. (ed.) *Stages of Social Research*. New Jersey, Prentice-Hall Inc.

WILLIAMS, K. (1978) Ideologies of Nursing. In: DINGWALL, R. and McINTOSH, J. *Readings in the Sociology of Nursing*. Edinburgh, Churchill Livingstone.

WILSON, K. (1975) *A Study of the Biological Sciences in Relation to Nursing*. Edinburgh, Churchill Livingstone.

WILSON-BARNETT, J. (1973) The Work of the Unit Nursing Officer. *Nursing Times,* **69**, (25) Occasional Paper (Part 1) 97–103.

WOODWARD, J. (1965) *Industrial Organisation Theory and Practice*. London, Oxford University Press.